Freedom, Emotion and Fascism

FREEDOM, EMOTION, AND FASCISM

A Psycho-Sociological Analysis of the
Modern American Progressive Movement

MARC SCHIFANELLI

LIBERTY HILL

Liberty Hill Publishing
2301 Lucien Way #415
Maitland, FL 32751
407.339.4217
www.libertyhillpublishing.com

Paperback ISBN-13: 978-1-6628-5179-7
Ebook ISBN-13: 978-1-6628-5263-3

Dedicated to those throughout history who saw it coming
and did all they could to stop it.

TABLE OF CONTENTS

"For liberty is like those solid and tasty foods or those full-bodied wines which are appropriate for nourishing and strengthening robust constitutions that are used to them, but which overpower, ruin and intoxicate the weak and delicate who are not suited for them."

– Jean Jacque Rousseau, *Discourse on the Origin and Foundation of Inequality Among Men,* 1755

"…the masses love the ruler rather than the suppliant, and inwardly they are far more satisfied by a doctrine which tolerates no rival than by the grant of liberal freedom: they often feel at a loss what to do with it, and even easily feel themselves deserted."

– Adolf Hitler, *Mein Kampf,* 1932

INTRODUCTION

"So don't think you can fool me with your political tricks
Political right, political left, you can keep your politics
Government is government and all government is force Left or
right, right or left, it takes the same old course
Oppression and restriction, regulation, rule and law
The seizure of that power is all your revolution's for
You romanticize your heroes, quote from Marx and Mao
Well their ideas of freedom are just oppression now..."

– Crass, *Bloody Revolutions*

The Modern American Progressive Movement

The American Progressive movement is approximately 150 years old. It began in the late 1800s as a reaction to the significant demographic shifts caused by the Industrial Revolution. Having started in Europe decades before, the Industrial Revolution in the United States was considered a "second wave" that began in earnest during the immediate post-Civil War era. Rapidly developing technology, mechanization, advances in science, and the increasingly efficient techniques of the division of labor and mass production resulted in cost-effective, profit-maximizing production of goods -goods that many Americans could for the first time afford to purchase.

Although mechanization of the production process increasingly replaced the need for some workers, the sheer growth and volume of American industry demanded labor and lots of it.

A large percentage of the required labor for growing factories and manufacturing plants came from rural America, as demographics shifted toward urban centers. Part of the impetus for this shift was the result of technological advances in agriculture. Just as factories had relied upon invention and ingenuity to reach increasingly efficient output by mass production, so too did agriculture. Developments in mechanical farming technology and agricultural science had been steadily improving crop, dairy, and farm production. This meant less hands were required to produce the same or even higher yield. Meanwhile, by the late 1800s U.S. government offers of "free land" in the American West – for those who had been willing to venture out to settle it – had ended. These changes resulted in less incentive or opportunity for unskilled labor living in rural America, and jobs in the expanding urban areas seemed a much better option for many, and many ultimately made the move from the countryside to the city. During the same era, new waves of immigrants – including many Irish fleeing famine, Southern Europeans, and Asians–disembarked at ports of entry in San Francisco and New York City. They came with high expectations in the land of opportunity, and of opportunity there was plenty. In a relatively short time, there arose an unprecedented industrial workforce in urban centers around the country.

Capitalism, the ethical-political doctrine that had been gradually coming to define the economic relations between men in Europe and then America during the centuries prior, was now trying to keep pace with revolutionary changes in production and in society. The major demographic shift from rural areas to urban, coupled with unprecedented waves of immigrants, created a large supply of unskilled labor for industry and ancillary businesses. In their efficiency, Capitalism and the free market economic system drove unskilled labor wages down. Consequently, industrial businesses were able to pay workers oppressively low wages–often barely enough to provide for subsistence. There was no legal minimum wage, and there was no legal minimum age. Additionally, working conditions and environments in factories and production houses were often hazardous, and with men and mechanical machines working in proximity, catastrophic accidents were predictable. When they occurred it wasn't usually the machine that came out with the short end. With no worker's compensation laws in effect, men, women, and sometimes children were cast aside to deal with their new physical deformities and handicaps without compensation. Often this meant having little or no means to feed themselves or their families. Even in cases where the employer was clearly at fault for his worker's injury, a worker typically had no ability to sue for compensation. Lawyer services required money, and industrial businesses could often outspend an injured plaintiff or use delaying tactics to attrit and discourage those few lawyers who might consider working on a contingency fee.

Arguably, had the Industrial Revolution not proceeded as 'revolutionary' as it did, i.e., had industrial technology and concepts of mass production occurred at a slower pace, the vast numbers of poor in cities across the United States and Europe may not have been so significant. Workers would have had more generational time to adapt and adjust to changes. As it was, the number of poor and unskilled labor in urban areas was staggering. So much so that in the 1880s a new

Progressive political movement had formed with the intention of ameliorating the conditions of the burgeoning class of poor and disaffected. Several American presidents of the era campaigned on "Progressive" social platforms, beginning with President Theodore Roosevelt. Roosevelt was elected on a "Progressive Party" platform, promising to introduce and sign into law "trust buster" legislation with the power to break up (and ultimately control) growing industrial giants. His successor, President Woodrow Wilson, continued Roosevelt's efforts at social reform during an era now referred to as "Wilsonian Progressivism." Progressive activists lobbied Congress to pass laws that called for worker protections. These included Federal Worker's Compensation in 1911, a concept adopted by the various states beginning in 1916, as well as restrictions on the use of child labor.

In the post-World War I era, Progressive efforts turned to creating a "socially just" society, and whereas the Progressive movement's original philosophical impetus had been the traditional "old liberal" concepts of equality and liberty, increasingly the movement adopted the relatively new tenets of Marxist communism. The 1917 October Revolution had caused Communism to gain international attention, particularly in Europe and the United States. Propaganda emanating from post-Tsarist Russia portrayed a nation of workers living the Utopian dream. All of them toiling for the collective and for the good of all. Ownership of the means of industry – capital – had been placed firmly in the hands of the workers, viz., in the hands of those who represented the workers: the new central government or local collectives.

In the United States during the 1920s, the Progressive movement inspired organized labor disputes, strikes, and riots. Using the recent Marxist "successes" in Russia as an ideal, organizers pitted workers against industry owners and management to demand better working conditions and wages. Often these disputes were met with excessive reactionary violence from state or local law enforcement, but they increased in frequency and pitch past the 1929 stock market crash and into the Great Depression. By the time President Franklin D. Roosevelt took office in 1933–himself having run on a Progressive platform–he was greatly concerned about the grassroots Marxist nature of the labor organizations and their activism. They could, he feared, win increasing popular support during the Depression years and thus gain more representation in government to promote Socialist ideology – something that was already happening in several European states, including Germany and Italy. In response, FDR sponsored legislation meant to not only allay the concerns and unrest of the American working class but also meant to decrease the growing influence of grassroots Marxism.

With many of its worker reform initiatives met since the turn of the Century, including the most recent social safety net provisions in Roosevelt's 1930s New Deal legislation, the trajectory of the Progressive movement petered out somewhat and became largely dormant. Marxist motivated labor strikes, protests, and reactionary suppression largely disappeared as well. Labor unions that had only recently championed Marxist ideology following the Russian Revolution, wound down their rhetoric. By the mid-1930s and with the Great Depression in full swing, America was focused more on getting its workers back *to* work, and not so much on the conditions *at* work. America's flirtation with Marxism seemed over, at least for now, but the early signs of war and worse in Europe would soon bring with them a new class of Marxists.

Throughout the 1930s, European Socialism had become a model to American Progressives, one openly admired by many American Democrat politicians. Social Utopia, many believed, could be achieved through Marxist Socialist theory, science, and strong leadership. Socialism would relegate to history the concept of being poor, each member of society producing "according to his ability," and every other member receiving his share "according to his needs." Science and technology could play their part through *social engineering*. Eugenics became a central philosophy of American Progressivism, calling for human heredity to be controlled by the government and not individual choice. That is, certain people with socially undesirable physical or mental traits should legally not be allowed to procreate. Those tending toward criminality, mental instability, or physical disability, could be prevented from passing on their undesirable gene pools. Genetic traits were likely (using Mendel's theory) to create children who themselves would only grow to become a drag on society. Progressive activist Margaret Sanger, the founder of Planned Parenthood and what she called the "Negro Project," advocated for legalizing abortion in order to achieve "the gradual suppression, elimination, and eventual extinction, of defective stocks — those human weeds which threaten the blooming of the finest flowers of American civilization." [1] This would be best for the collective good and therefore ethical, and both abortion and forced sterilization were useful tools to this end. [2]

Progressives revered strong leaders like Adolf Hitler and Mussolini for their avant-garde, visionary social engineering plans to "clean up" Europe. By 1932, the German Parliament was comprised of a majority of Socialists. Hitler, the leader of the German Socialist Worker's Party ("Nazi" Party), was appointed Chancellor that same year. Whereas the Russian Revolution had ushered in a philosophy of socialist collectivism administered by a Communist political system, one that demanded individual subservience to "the masses," German Socialism chose instead to rely upon a system of fascism and demanding individual subservience for the collective good of the German people and race. Hitler preferred the leftist nature of Socialist Fascism to that of Communism, the systems only separated by a few degrees, for pragmatic reasons. Whereas Communism's theory of collectivism required government ownership of industry, as well as farms and other means of production, Hitler was content to leave these to private ownership which, with the profit motive left intact, he knew would be much more efficient than under collective ownership and control. As long as the results of private industry benefitted the nationalist cause, including military and economic might, this was acceptable. In this, he differed from the Communists, whose doctrine and activism Hitler would not tolerate.

For many others, however, the Socialist Fascist rhetoric coming out of Hitler's Germany and Italy clearly foreshadowed something evil. For the German Jews, things were becoming incrementally worse. Hitler's disdain of the Jews, singling them out as domestic enemies of the German people and the Aryan race, had been since 1932 no secret. The German people zealously accepted Hitler's scapegoating of them, while the Socialist-controlled German Parliament passed antisemitic laws, one after the other, beginning as early as 1933. Popular boycotts of Jewish-owned businesses coupled with the antisemitic legislation made life, at best, progressively challenging for them. Although many Jews continued to live in denial – believing that things could not get much worse–many others saw the writing on the wall. Ironically, this included a handful of hardcore Marxist political philosophers and academics, all of them German Jews. Fearing for their lives as both Jews in the now Socialist Fascist Germany and knowing Hitler's disdain for the Socialist Communists, especially the Com Intern, [3] they fled socialist Germany for the safety of Capitalist America. Once in the United States, they could ponder, write about, and spread with little interference what was becoming a very appealing gospel: the gospel of Collectivism and Communism. Their collaborative efforts at putting Marxist Communism into practice was their central focus and it was not long after their arrival in America before they acquired the title of the "Frankfurt School."[4]

Karl Marx had theorized that before the Communist system could become reality, Capitalism would first need to fully develop itself. Eventually, however, the Capitalist system would collapse under its own 'contradictions' between the workers and the owners of capital, i.e., the wealthy. This collapse would cause a spontaneous, revolutionary spirit or consciousness among the working class who would rise up in revolt, moving nations, and the world to their ultimate state of social Utopia. The collapse of Capitalism was, for Marx, a necessary step in the movement and was known as "scientific Marxism."

The Frankfurt School philosophers, however, had their own theory of how Marxist Socialist Communism could take hold in America and eventually throughout the world. They weren't keen on waiting for Capitalism to fall apart on its own "contradictions," and to all indications, this didn't seem to be happening. They believed that the necessary "revolutionary consciousness [could] be achieved without the incremental development called for by scientific Marxism." [5] In other words, a Capitalist society could make an end-run around the scientific process by instigating a revolutionary spirit through conflict, not between oppressed working poor and the capitalistic wealthy (classic Marxist Conflict Theory), but by creating conflict among other non-economic classes, exploiting their identities in order to create social division and then revolution. Race, ethnicity, religion, sex, and gender could be made to serve as the basis for identity group versus identity group conflict. This focus on immutable, non-economic characteristics became known as Cultural Marxism or "Critical Theory."

During World War II, when Americans went back to work in record numbers and the Great Depression became relegated to history, American Progressivism made little headway in social reform legislation. The subsequent American economic boom that followed the War not only nurtured a "Baby Boom" Generation, but it helped foster the image of the American Dream as one surrounded by a suburban, "blue collar" lifestyle, and economically optimistic. In the strong post-War economy, most people were doing relatively well. The American Middle Class appeared on the scene, and the American Dream and the freedom to pursue it were within reach of the vast majority. Family vacations were now something for the new middle and upper-middle classes–no longer limited to the wealthier classes. Resorts opened where families could come and forget the travails of life for a while or a weekend. Most everyone could afford both a family car and then a television set. The need for social change or the ideal of "social justice" – such as it had been driven by the economic disparity of a class of poor in dire conditions before the War – lost its popular appeal in a period of economic prosperity in which everyone seemed to benefit. Furthermore, the modern, economically thriving America was engaged in a new Cold War rivalry with the Communist Soviet Union. Mainstream Americans saw Communism as clearly inapposite of American values – both in theory and in practice. Labor disputes still arose, and in the post-war era of unprecedented economic strength, unions and union membership exploded and its bargaining power with management increased proportionally. However, both sides of any labor dispute in the post-War era, and unlike those of the pre-War era, agreed that Capitalism, and not Communism, was the preferred social system. That was beyond dispute.

Consequently, American Progressivism and its Marxist ideology took a backseat in American Post-War politics. The two-party system that included the Republican and Democrat parties largely satisfied the political ideological needs of most American voters on a more or less fifty/fifty basis. But underneath the surface, particularly in academia, things began to change as several different social and political philosophies began to interact and influence each other. A school of thought had early emerged with a "post-modern," nihilist philosophy of life and politics, i.e., that nothing in the world has any real existence or meaning. This philosophy was rooted in the epistemological argument that true knowledge, i.e., knowledge based on facts that are objectively verifiable and justifiable, is simply impossible. In other words, that which may be true according to one person's personal and subjective experience could at the same time be false according to another's subjective experience. Since nothing could ever be determined as factual, nothing could really be true or false. Objective knowledge, for the post-modernist, was unknowable, definitive knowledge impossible, and facts simply could not be verified through objectivity, logical analysis, and reason. Only "true knowledge" is valid, and true knowledge is achieved only through individual subjectivity: based on a person's experiences. Thus, every person can have a different "true knowledge" and so for any given argument, two people can both be right even if their factual conclusions are mutually exclusive. They were, in short, trying to prove that nothing can be proved and that facts and knowledge are, in fact, unknowable.

With such glaring contradictions, post-modernist philosophy did not find much popularity and eventually subsided after some vigorous debate. However, many university professors in academia had gotten hooked on it. They saw in it an opportunity to apply it the contemporary social issues that faced American society.[6] For example, in the late 1970s, Progressive legal scholars began criticizing the U.S. legal system, its laws, and the basis of American jurisprudence (the theory of law generally and its *universal* premises and applications). These, they professed, were blatant tools of power and oppression created and used by the dominant socio-economic classes of American society (i.e., white Western males) to oppress the non-dominant classes. [7] Police power, economic policies, Capitalism, the rights guaranteed and protected by the U.S. Constitution, and so on, were simply tools designed by the rich to oppress the poor. And as the rich were, they professed, "white Anglo Saxon Protestants," these tools were racist, misogynist, and exclusive, meant only to keep WASPs in power. These legal scholars founded *Critical Legal Studies* which would later branch into many sub-studies or "critical theories," including *Feminist Law Studies* and *Critical Race Law/Critical Race Theory*. Critical Legal Studies maintained a clear connection to Marxist

Socialism as their "most direct philosophical antecedent..." [8] More specifically, the "Crits" (as these new scholars became known) had infused their post-modern theories with the theories of the Frankfurt School and Critical Marxism.

By the mid-1980s, *Critical Race* and *Feminist Law* theory began to get wider attention in academic circles. Critical Feminists lamented that "male logic" infused all Western legal thought. Male logic, they contended, relied only on objectivity and neutrality, leaving no space for "female logic" to make its own mark. [9] Critical Feminists argued that "male logic" relied on objective, verifiable knowledge, or other "male" concepts like *"unsituated knowledge,"* and l *"uniformity and sameness."* [10] Peculiarly female legal perspectives, they contended, included concepts such as "openness, inclusivity, and equal respect..." [11] (How concepts such as openness, equal respect, and inclusivity became strictly feminine attributes is a mystery). Consequently, men had developed the ideas in Western jurisprudence without ever having consulted their biological counterpart's rules of logic. Therefore, Feminist Crits concluded, Western law was obviously discriminatory against women.

For the Critical Race Theory and Critical Race Law proponents, equal treatment under the law could never be attained because Western law was created by an oppressor class – i.e., Europeans and, in America, the colonial Framers of the Constitution–and forced upon the oppressed classes. Unless and until white Americans acknowledged that it was because of their implicit bias and racism that black Americans had made what they (erroneously) perceived to be zero progress in personal wealth and social status since Emancipation, black Americans would remain oppressed. Individual whites were only successful in life because their race is inequitably reinforced by Western, "colonial" institutions of oppression: the nuclear family, education focusing on logic and objective reasoning, Capitalism and Individualism, and a strong sense of self-reliance (what Critical Race advocates derogatorily call "the Bootstrap Theory") to name just a few.

These new "Crit" theories were at first welcomed for debate in academia – just what one would expect of any novel political or social theories. Legal scholars considered Crit theories and opened them up for wide debate. Soon, many began to see flaws in the theories. The chief complaint was that the new Crit theorists often philosophized and wrote from subjective, not objective, points of view: they often inserted their own personal experiences as premises to support what they considered to be universal conclusions of modern jurisprudence. This fallacy was so prevalent in the new critical theories that serious scholars began to refer to the entire body of Crit theory pejoratively as "narrative jurisprudence." Furthermore, as the Critical Race Law advocates specifically, many considered that they "reveal[ed] other deficiencies–a tendency to evade or suppress complications that render their conclusions problematic. Stated bluntly, they fail to support persuasively their claims of racial exclusion or their claims that legal academic scholars of color produce a racially distinctive band of valuable scholarship..." In effect, the Crits were attempting to develop theories of law based on the culture of various identity groups, for example, the gay and lesbian community, one's race or sex, and later one's gender "identity," as opposed to a jurisprudence that considered humanity as a whole. [12]

When crit theories began to come under heavy intellectual fire – their arguments questioned for their non-universal application or for their anecdotal nature the debate took a turn.

Scholars were shut down (and often too easily folded out of fear) by *ad hominem* attacks and defamatory attacks on their reputations. Crits and their supporters vehemently accused and labeled those who disagreed with them as bigoted, racist misogynists, "offensive" or–simply because of their sex or skin color–unqualified to present any argument in opposition to the new critical theories. This was the beginning of "cancel culture" and protests against any professor or academic accused of racism, "homophobia," or other such characteristics often resulted in termination by weak, hypersensitive university directors and boards. By the mid-1980s "political correctness" was quickly and effectively chilling speech and the marketplace of ideas. Many otherwise innocent people lost their positions, jobs, and reputations as a result of mob 'justice.'

With the hurdle of intellectual public discourse and debate out of the way, Critical and other postmodern theories and concepts raced to popularity, their soundness and validity left unchallenged out of fear. Amenable university professors increasingly integrated the tenets of critical theories into their teaching. Baby Boomers who had been young, impressionable students of those first post-modernist professors, themselves now became professors. Those who had found credence in post-modernist thought further 'refined' it for themselves and their students. The exponential increase in university-level professors and academics influenced by original post-modernism and now critical theories increased their popularity and distribution. They continued to seep into more analyses of the salient social issues of the day with the objective of remedying social inequalities. Modern Progressives both inside and outside of academia became more and more enamored with new, subjective, and "experienced-based" theories, especially since any fact or logic-based arguments in opposition could be snuffed out by attacking the opponent instead of her argument.

The result was an emerging American Progressive Movement intent on resolving social and political issues with unchallenged theoretical and philosophical foundations: foundations loosely formed with subjectivity, contradiction, conflicting factual bases, and – as is constantly demonstrated in modern Progressive arguments–hypocrisy. Progressives found they could effectively rely on appeals to emotion to justify the application of these theories in the public arena. And emotion is inherently a powerful motivator of human behavior and decision making. For the modern American Progressive, the more that the subjective critical theories activated his emotions, the more emotion he fed back into his search for explanations to the world's problems, developing more subjective theories to that end.

Because the cultural *oppressor-oppressed* framework was so handy for Progressives in promoting critical law and feminist studies other theories rapidly sprouted from it. For example, Leftist academics developed Critical Gender Theory and Queer Theory. They produced the theory of "intersectionalism" – the notion that one's "individual" identity is not determined by one's unique character and personality traits, but by the type and number of "identity groups" to which she could lay claim as a member. By the end of the Twentieth Century, crit academics were trying to explain a whole range of what was 'normal' in the human condition. For example, *critical fat theory* attempted to explain that being overweight, even obese, was a natural and desirable state of which the person should be proud. [13] Overweight people were simply stigmatized, argued the Progressive, by a paradigm of oppression created by oppressor white males that obesity was unhealthy— that the ideal human body should resemble something more fit. Anyone who was obese and tried to lose weight? They were a traitor to the new identity group of fat people and only acted that way in submission to white male preferences – even if it was their doctor who recommended that they lose weight for health reasons. [14]

Feminism began to turn fascistic as the up-and-coming post-modern feminists demanded conformity to the new critical gender theories, ousting the old-guard feminists along with their antiquated view that feminism was something more spiritually profound than just blaming men for all of womankind's modern problems (which for the new feminists now included the inherent oppressor-oppressed dynamic in sexual intercourse).[15]

Often referred to as "woke" or "wokism," modern Progressivism exhibits a renewed emphasis on social justice and the redistribution of wealth and power. Progressives fuel activism in education as well as politics. [16] Recently, Progressive academics and school professionals convinced students that they need "safe spaces" where they may be shielded from Conservative or Libertarian arguments that "offend" them. Arguments in favor of say individual rights, such as unrestricted freedom of speech, religious freedom, or a citizen's right to bear arms without asking government for permission to do so, are prohibited in the Progressive's safe space. These notions are contrary to the Progressive's collectivist ideology: in Utopia people cannot engage in "hate speech." Hate is after all a bad emotion that can cause people to do harmful things. And guns can be used by hateful people. Hence, hate speech should be banned, and guns are a small thing to give up in the name of peace and protection of the collective. In 2022, Georgetown law students demanded that the school administration provide them a designated safe space where they could "cry" after an incoming lecturer criticized President Biden's declaration that he would only nominate black female justices to replace Justice Breyer on the U.S. Supreme Court. [17]

For those whom Jean Jacques Rousseau considered "weak and fragile" in the face of liberty, safe spaces are arguably little intellectual prisons in which young Progressives may sit. The intent and the effect are to keep out any thought that challenges their shaky Progressive political and social theories. Led to believe that the spaces are of the young students' own making, they are really meant to protect Progressive academia's collective ego. Since no opposing perspective that challenges, say, the shaky philosophical tenets of Critical Race Theory, can reach her, the student feels safe against "implicit racism," but the academic is even more content in the knowledge that the emperor still appears clothed.

While truly intellectual conversations thus go on without them, Progressives prefer to classify themselves and each other–not by their intellectual ability or individual achievements–but by "affirming" themselves through identity group association. They "self-identify" as part of this or that group that shares an immutable characteristic like their skin color, ethnicity, or sex, or by a subjective (and largely intellectually irrelevant) idea of gender identity. Reliance on the superficial leads to what they believe are intellectual arguments that cannot be challenged, yet in reality have little substantive use. To add more credence to the arguments that they make the attempt to add combinations of these reflective identities, or "intersections." My argument is right, a Progressive might assert in the converse of *ad hominem* because I am a disabled, bisexual, male "Latinx." It's like the pretentious college professor who ultimately defends her weak argument by saying with finality, "This argument is valid and sound because I'm the professor and you are not." If you still disagree? Well, there goes your GPA.

When hate-sounding speech does happen to get through their cage bars, the new Progressives consider this as the equivalent of a violent assault. Conservative speech is "violence" and young social justice radicals have again been led by Progressive mentors to believe that physical violence is justified in the face of what they consider the violence of non-Marxist ideals. Anyone perceived as not conforming to their new social justice theories is targeted for retaliation to shut them up. Leading up to and after the 2016 election, Progressives and "social justice warriors" engaged in hundreds of acts of violence aimed at Republicans, conservatives, and anyone perceived to be right of the political center. "Get up in their face," Progressive politicians told their followers after the post-election riots had subsided, and this they did.

Like the Socialist Fascist Brown and Black Shirts of pre-War Europe, modern Progressives realize that physical violence is effective in shutting down opposition voices. Like Maoists, they also know the power of just the *idea* of violence. With an arguably sadistic need to control others who do not share their ideals, the Progressive has found that destroying a person's livelihood is also an effective means to create terror in a vocal enemy. Attacks on private individuals by means of reputational harm with the intent to have them lose their employment, position, or livelihoods began with conservative academics in the 1980s but have increased in scope. "Cancel culture" and "doxing" are new terms that cause anxiety in people who want to say what they really think but won't dare out of fear. Cancelling now includes not only boycotting a popular star or public personality for their professed or perceived world views but going after everyday individuals to crush them. Calls, emails, texts, social media posts, letters – an employer is notified that he or she has in their employ a racist, homophobe, misogynist, etc. Many employers cave, some quite easily, and fire the targeted person or ask for their resignation rather than have their businesses 'tarnished' by what they perceive is much of the public. This is simple terrorism – harming one person for her speech in order to cause fear of speaking in a thousand other people–and many have succumbed to it for fear of being the next target of the defamation mob.

The modern Progressive admires what they perceive as the "righteous" use of strong government power and authority: forcing a small family baker to bake a $50 cake for a gay marriage ceremony–something that goes against his sincerely held religious beliefs – for a gay couple. Crucify him, they say. Drag him into court and bankrupt him with attorney's fees and boycotts. The Progressives elected to local government used their power to fine the baker in support of the couple, and when the Supreme Court of the United States finally overturns their rulings and actions as unconstitutional, the Progressives' deep-seated need to force the baker to conform resurfaces and they bait and target him again.

While striving to establish a more authoritarian and controlling one-party government, Progressives in what can only be described as a simultaneously sadistic and masochistic desire wish for totalitarian control over the nation while urging its destruction by erasing its geopolitical borders. They praise the establishment of an amorphous, submissive area with no borders–one subsumed and subservient to global power. They applaud the entry of anyone who wants to come in unlawfully and with whatever motivation, economic or criminal. This yearning for both a strong authoritarian state while at the same time yearning for that state's submission and ultimate demise is indicative of a confused ideology that would cut off its nose to spite its face that wishes for its own destruction to guarantee its life.

Seemingly with a masochistic desire for emotional pain, American Progressives regularly blame themselves for the enslavement of Africans in the United States between 1776 and 1865. They loudly claim that they (and everybody else) need to pay for the sins of those who came before in a convoluted attempt at a moral consanguine obligation. America and its economy, they say seemingly with little understanding of economics, was built on slavery. The Constitution itself is inherently racist because a fraction of the hundred or so of the Nation's Framers owned slaves. Because of that, the Constitution is a tool of white oppression and needs to be scrapped (using this same logic, Penicillin would need to be scrapped if it were found that Alexander Fleming favored racial segregation after the Civil War). They chastise and emotionally flog themselves for their "white privilege" and confess their "guilt" for being a member of a race that over a hundred and forty years ago enslaved others of another race.

"Daily," wrote one blue-collar Progressive on her social media page, "I reap the benefits of my white skin and struggle to overcome my racism." Professing proudly to be "anti-racist," they cannot see past the color of a person's skin, no clue as to the potential individual and intellectual beauty that might lay beneath it. Rather, they embrace the notion that if someone of color should reveal any intellectual individualism, i.e., conservative thought, then the person is a "race traitor," a "white ally," or an "Uncle Tom." Ellen DeGeneres jokes while getting a fast piggyback ride from a black track star by saying (paraphrasing), "This is how I'm doing my shopping from now on," and is attacked in the most debasing terms by emotional Progressives who are unable to see a professional entertainer having fun with a professional athlete. They are capable only of seeing a white woman exploiting a black man. Progressives are simply not allowed to be "color blind" or see the true joy in life and human interaction.

Progressives have been convinced that certain people can be guilty of 'cultural misappropriation' and are now even criminally responsible for "cultural *theft*" if they copy or use certain cultural symbols or customs originating from an ethnic group not their own. Although these cultural customs are not 'owned' by anyone in any even remote legal sense, this makes little difference. For example, non-Indian Yoga teachers are vehemently accused by American Progressives, mostly non-Indian, of shamefully misappropriating an Indian custom and tradition for their own economic benefit. A maintenance worker of Jamaican ethnicity attacks a white student on a college campus for having his long hair in *dreadlocks* – yelling at him that he has committed "cultural misappropriation" from Jamaicans (apparently without realizing that Jamaicans, and more accurately Rastafarians, adopted the style from Ethiopia warriors of an earlier era). That the maintenance worker wears Levi jeans – an American cultural symbol created by a Jew – escapes her as what would logically be a double standard application of the cultural theft concept, except that Progressives have promoted the concept as only applying when the cultural symbol "stolen" has origins in a minority group. Narrow minds, like narrow streets it seems, are only suited for one-way traffic.

With seemingly no idea of what money is, much less how it works, they yearn for Universal Basic Income. "[Y]es," says a young Progressive on social media, "universal basic income would allow us to survive between jobs but it would also allow us to grieve, after loss, to move, to care for others, to have children, to create art, to start new businesses, to be ill, to be disabled, to rest, to rest, to rest…" [18] Her several hundred Twitter followers seem perplexed as to how mankind even made it to 2022 *without* Universal Basic Income.

Attempting to wrest control of science and relying on nihilism, Progressives believe humans can have more than two biological sexes, men can have babies and "chest feed" if that's how they want to "identify," and a woman from a Nordic race can dye her skin and thus identify as a black American. In the name of "fairness," they advocate for the imposition of biological males to compete with women in high school and college sports, seemingly unable to accept that women are generally less muscular than men while the latter set new records for women's sports and to the glee and utter amazement of the Progressive. With reality dysphoria, the Progressive has no idea of the damage he is doing to young women in sports who pursue recognition and scholarships that come with winning or placing higher in a competition amongst their peers and without having to compete in wrestling, swimming, or sprinting with biological males.

In a social charade whose equal can only be found in fairytale, Progressives are convinced they are being more egalitarian, more "inclusive" of others and each other if they create their own identity language. They have spent their time inventing pronouns to replace "himself" and "herself" with new options that include "pirself," "hirself," "verself," and "zirself."[19] This identifying is supposed to give the young person a new lens through which they can view the world differently and therefore become more well-rounded, more knowledgeable about pirself. "'It maximizes the student's ability to control their identity,'" said Keith Williams, the University of Vermont Registrar "who helped to launch the updated student information system in 2009."[20] When and if they snap out of it with maturity, they are no wiser to the reality of the world than when they started.

After the 2016 Presidential Election upset, Progressives self-diagnosed with "Trump Derangement Syndrome" to such an emotional degree that mental health professionals were compelled to give the syndrome legitimacy. A large portion of the American Progressive Left was, in fact, having severe emotional distress as a result of it. Universities set up emergency mental health facilities with therapeutic props like furry animal dolls, live pets, and other items. Assistance was made available to alleviate distress among their Progressive student populations. Progressive voters sobbed or screamed uncontrollably that "this is our country" and the winner was "not my president." Progressives in Portland who were angry with the election results came out to riot, burn and loot, resulting in local law enforcement arresting at least one hundred adults. To their surprise, over half of them were not even registered to vote.

Meanwhile, American Progressives in public schools, teachers, and administrators, demand that public Kindergarten children be exposed to books with titles like "The Hips on the Drag Queen Go Swish, Swish, Swish" written by Lil' Miss Hot Mess – apparently with social engineering motives but arguably a form of sexual predation and grooming.[21] "It is great and quite normal," they believe, that men with lipstick and bras read these books in school media centers so kindergarteners can learn to be more gender "inclusive." They provide students with books complete with lewd and lascivious graphics of children engaging in sexual acts while citing the book's "literary" value, scientific value, and the "creation of empathy," a human emotion existing long before Lil' Miss Hot Mess. [22] When parents of these public schoolchildren complained to their local Boards of Education, a Progressive president of the National School Boards Association (NSBA) appealed to the president of the United States to brand them as "domestic terrorists." [23]

When Americans stop to contemplate the modern American Progressive, they ask themselves, "*Are these people crazy*?!"

Is the Modern American Progressive Really Crazy?

Posed in this way the question may seem unacademic. For starters, the word "crazy" is probably not the most clinical of terms. This does not, however, make the question invalid and by no means irrelevant. As evidenced by those Progressives who sought psychological relief for "Trump Derangement Syndrome" or who regularly demand "safe spaces" in which certain political philosophy or social thought cannot enter for fear of causing intense emotional pain, there is something in the acts of the individual American Progressive and in the collective psyche of the movement that seems queer. There seems to be an *emotional fragility* that pervades the reasoning of the Progressive and characterizes the Progressive Movement overall: an overreliance on emotion generally and an overemphasis on several particular emotions. When faced with realities that do not conform with the Progressive worldview, they are easily frazzled to the point of emotional outbursts, sobbing, lashing out with physical violence, or intimidation by *cancelling* and *doxing*. Increasingly, the word "psychosis" appears in social media posts and media outlet commentary to describe not only the psychology behind these emotionally charged behaviors but the *psyche* of the Movement overall.

Modern Progressivism is synonymous with Marxist Socialism. Progressives support Socialist concepts such as Universal Basic Income, and command economic programs like the Congressional Progressive Caucus' "People's Budget." They are quick to limit or deny individual rights if they believe it is best for the common good, e.g., the right to gun ownership (in order to, as Hillary Clinton phrased it, "save the toddlers"). They solicit support for these and other Socialist policies in the name of inherently vague ethical notions such as "fairness" and "equity" that can mean different things to different people (including impartial and trained judges). They appeal to false notions of "guilt" and stretch the virtue of self-sacrifice to the point of *loss of self* to the Collective.

"To be a socialist," wrote Simone de Beauvoir, "is to submit the I to the thou, socialism is sacrificing the individual to the whole."[24] In the name of "more freedom" and "more choice," Progressives paradoxically surrender their individual freedom in deference to this more powerful, more controlling, more authoritarian "whole" or collective. Willingly ceding one's individual freedom and individual self to Collective rule is, *de facto*, the suicidal destruction of the individual and the self.

And the desire to destroy oneself is, after all, an indicator of mental illness.

In 1941, psychoanalyst and sociologist Erich Fromm published what was one of the first comprehensive studies of the psychology underlying the rise of the Nationalist Socialist ("Nazi") movement in Germany. His book, *Escape from Freedom*, analyzed the behavioral characteristics not only of Hitler (an analysis that the U.S. Office of Strategic Services had also secretly done) but also of the German people. It was they who had been receptive to the Nazi ideology, a people for whom Hitler's socialist fascism had an obvious and vigorous appeal. Fromm used his experience in psychoanalysis to analyze Hitler's 1938 book, *Mein Kampf*, which had by the end of that decade become a best-seller with more than one million copies sold. He also focused on Hitler's impassioned speeches. These seemed to electrify, awe, and in some cases incense the German people to collective action. It was this relationship, Fromm believed, between Hitler's Nazi Party doctrines and the German people to whom these doctrines so deeply appealed that was the key to understanding how socialist Fascism in Germany and in Europe, including in Italy and Spain, had come to be such a powerful force.

Fromm was not the only sociologist assessing the rise of Fascism in Europe. Fascism was a political system novel in its modern form, and it had captured the interests of political analysts who viewed, considered, and argued its merits in European and American academic circles. In the 1930s, American Progressives especially admired men like Adolf Hitler. To them, Hitler was a visionary who was "cleaning up" Europe using cutting-edge social engineering, including *eugenics*. For example, attempting to engineer modern society in order to rid it of social deviants, criminals, and the poor, all of whom, Progressives believed, were incapable of education and thus of living productive lives for the benefit of collective society. "Appeasement" was the diplomatic doctrine in relation to Germany's growing geographical aspirations, but, thought Progressives, how bad could things get if Hitler was only making European society better?

Concomitant with the rise of Socialist Fascism, contemporary political scientists and sociologists had also been studying Marxist Communism, and not just in the theoretical or philosophical sense. Since 1917 when the Communists implemented one-party rule in post-Revolution Russia, effectively putting the Communist "Utopian" political theory into practice, analysts were finally able to critique how Marx's Socialist Communist philosophy worked in practice. Along with its chief and founding advocate in post-Tsarist Russia, Vladimir Lenin, they quickly discovered that for Communism to work, violence was a necessity. The Utopian principles that Marx had so faithfully laid out with Engels in his Communist Manifesto and in Das Kapital, i.e., that men would willingly give up their individual interests and pursuits and become subservient to the Collective – the working "masses"–who would equitably provide *the most good for the most people*...didn't seem to work without physical or mental coercion.

War ultimately did break out in 1939 with Fascist Italy and Nazi Germany as Axis belligerents in a war for the domination of Europe and beyond. After years of fighting on an unprecedented scale across the globe, the Allied front began to close in on Germany proper, and the horrific atrocities that the Fascists had been visiting upon their own people (and those in the conquered territory) began to receive international attention. Many outsiders who had observed the rise of European Fascism had from the beginning argued that, because of its obvious oppression of individual freedom, Fascism as a political system must have been *forced* upon the people. The Germans, for example, must have been coerced through fear and terror, bullied against their collective will to accept and support it. It could be no other way, they believed, but the result of a brutal single-party political movement–Hitler's Nazi Party and his henchmen–Goebbels, Himmler, and notorious others–who had evidently terrorized the Germans into supporting Socialist Fascism, while brutally stamping out any opposition to it.

Fromm, however, realized something to the contrary. He found that the majority of the German population had quite *willingly*, even zealously, supported Hitler and the Nazi movement. There was something in the relationship between the people and the Nazi doctrine that had resonated strongly that had motivated millions to not only passively support it, but to join the movement as "cogs in the wheel" of the Nazi machinery: as the National Socialist Party members, members of the German SS, the Gestapo secret police, or to volunteer for service in the expanding German military. Hitler had seemingly and quite easily convinced the German people that they, the Aryan race, were destined to defeat their enemies – enemies that he alleged lay all around them. It was simply a matter of power and control, and Germany had a moral obligation to rule over all other, weaker human races. To attain this destiny, Hitler demanded that the German people submit unconditionally to his Nationalist Socialist Party and its doctrine of intolerance. This they did and with little or no coercion.[25]

In looking at this mass act of willing submission, Fromm considered that,

> *"[t]he influence of any doctrine or idea depends on the extent to which it appeals to the psychic needs in the character structure of those to whom*

it is addressed. Only if the idea answers powerful psychological needs of certain social groups will it become a potent force in history." [26]

In other words, political and social ideas and ideals have the propensity to affect deeply held, often unconscious emotional needs. Hence, analyzing a social or political doctrine in and of itself is never sufficient to fully understand why or how it can be readily accepted by a portion of a given society. Identifying the psychological motivators of the character or personality type to whom the doctrine appeals is also necessary. Why are some people attracted, sometimes fanatically so, to social and political doctrines that compel them to action, even if that action is self-destructive to themselves, their families, their community, and their nation? If enough individuals find some type of solace in a political or social doctrine, then that doctrine could be identified as satisfying the psychological or "psychic" needs, not only of the individual but of the larger group or movement made up of those types of individuals: a group psyche. If the group is significant, then the doctrine will become one of those "potent forces" to which Fromm referred. That Nationalist Socialism as embodied in the Nazi Party's Fascist doctrine did appeal to and satisfy some psychic need or needs of the German people is beyond question. Clearly, Nazism did become that "potent force in history" and a highly self-destructive one. Although Hitler could be extremely charismatic in his delivery of the Nazi ideology, still it was the ideology, the doctrine itself that enticed the German people into following the Party's lead, ultimately to their own self-destruction and the destruction of the nation. In his analysis, Fromm went on to argue that the "deep psychic needs" of the German people were answered by what he characterized as a *sado-masochistic* relationship between the willingly submissive German people and the authoritarian Nazi Party doctrine. It was a relationship that demanded the German individual's strict subservience to the control of the Socialist collective, the state, and for the national glory of the German race.

This book considers the political psychology of the modern American Progressive for whom Marxism, Fascism, and Communism appear to have overwhelming emotional appeal. That is, what deep emotional needs of would-be Marxists, today represented in the politics of the American Progressive, does the idea of Collectivism in whatever form satisfy? What motivates the modern American Progressive to actively promote or passively support Collectivist social platforms, often under the facade of "social justice," zealously and increasingly with harmful intent and even violence? These questions are no less important today for Americans than they have ever been. As the American Progressive movement leads the American political Left and the Democrat Party further into Socialism through one-party rule, understanding what emotional needs Socialist political doctrines satisfy, including both Fascism and Communism, in the Progressive and his or her supporters is essential to combating its rise. Understanding the emotional, "psychic needs" of the Modern American Progressive, including those who both actively and passively support it, may yield insight into how those emotional needs may be allayed in order to avoid the historically self-destructive road from Socialism to Fascism, Communism, and inevitably, Totalitarianism.

The first several chapters are concerned with defining with more clarity collectivism in its various forms, including the true collectivist foundations of both Nationalist Socialism as well as Communist, and their destructive natures. It also discusses the concept of "individual freedom" – freedom that Americans more so than any other nation in history have experienced and continue to experience, often without more than a superficial understanding of what it means even though we "know it when we see it." The next chapter discusses political psychology and the role of emotion in political decision-making. This is followed by discussions of several emotions, namely envy, fear, and "guilt" (and as that term is employed by Progressive "social justice" advocates). Lastly, is a discussion and comparison with that overarching, potentially syndromic relationship that Fromm had identified in 1941 – of sadomasochism and the sadomasochistic relationship between those who willingly give up their individualism, rights, and freedoms in exchange for service and subservience what they perceive as a more powerful entity, i.e. the Collective.

Scope, Sources, and Methods

Categorizing anything, not least of all people, can often confound as much as it clarifies. However, political psychology has made major advances since the time Fromm wrote his analysis of the rise of Fascist Socialism in Nazi Germany. While this book does ultimately discuss and refer to several psychological concepts and disorders, it does not attempt to make any psychological determinations of mental illness or disorders in individual Progressives. It makes no claim of psychological diagnoses since the appropriate focus of psychoanalysis and psychological disorders can only be considered in the context of the unique circumstances of individual persons. Further, accusations of psychological disorders have been used before to discredit and attack political opponents, political enemies, competing social movements, rival social and ethnic groups, or simply the "socially undesirable" in communities throughout history. It's the "cheap shot" and an ad hominin argument at best, but it's one that has facilitated and sanctioned murder and torture.

Yet, to the extent that the emotional needs discussed herein are often prominently present in the psychological makeup of a certain character type – one to whom Fascism and Communism appeal–it is fair to also analyze whether a social movement, here the Modern American Progressive Movement if made up of a sufficient number of members who share that character type or who present observable behavioral indicators, can exhibit a collective psyche that defines the Movement's goals, its incentives, and its modus operandi. If these are in the aggregate ultimately destructive of the individual's spiritual and even physical existence, then it may be possible to view this collective psyche as a mass disorder akin to other phenomena, like "group think," or even, and as is used more and more by observers of the current Progressive Movement, as a "mass psychosis." Identifying common underlying emotions that tend to influence an individual's support for (or aversion to) a particular political ideology, doctrine, or platform, however, is much sounder. Given the unintended consequences that accompany any social or political mass movement, it is a subject that deserves consideration.

Hence, this book identifies and discusses *at least several of the potential emotional needs that make Socialist, collectivist platforms so appealing to Progressive Movement supporters: needs that are apparent in their public discourse, behavior, and their overt acts.* The focus herein is not on Marxist Socialism or neo-Marxism *per se*. Neither is it specifically a study of Fascism and Communism, the only two authoritarian political systems capable of administering a socialist society. It is strictly on answering the question what is it within the American Progressive that drives him or her toward collectivism?

Studies in psychology and sociology have shown that humans, being uniquely political animals, make political decisions often motivated by emotion, and people join social and political movements through an array of different motivations be they religious, political, social, radical, or conservative.

Humans also have another unique emotional capability. As a result of our ability to empathize with others, we can often decipher another's emotional state by, for example, the way they act or their posture as we talk to them. Sometimes we can "read" the expression on their face or in their eyes (what some call "the window to the brain"). Perhaps their *avoiding* eye contact with us can be an indicator of how or what they are feeling. Even though they may make statements to the contrary, their body language can reveal to us something about their true emotional state. And the same is applicable to not only the statements they make orally but in their written statements. "Reading between the lines" is a phrase that is often invoked when a listener or reader is giving another's statements more than superficial analysis. It's an attempt to comprehend the speaker's true meaning, intent, or motivation for making a statement or argument in favor or opposition to prospective policies or legislation.

And social media has revolutionized communications. The advent of the internet and its prolific usage by people from all walks of life and worldviews allow people–friends, "friends," acquaintances, and strangers to freely discuss and debate political issues quite easily. Arguments between users can result in explicit position statements, each side submitting their respective reasoning in favor or in opposition. Each side's reasoning can be held up to the rules of formal logic to assess the validity and soundness of the argument. Facts used to support an argument can be challenged, accepted, or "fact-checked."

If not censored, such social media posts and engagements can shed light on and reveal an author's deeper motivation for supporting one platform or the other. Often one can decipher the more profound, emotional psychology behind one's support or opposition to a political or social issue. Sometimes subtly or not so subtly, people can reveal the emotional basis for their investment in certain issues. Hence, much can be learned about the political psychology of the average American and, for purposes here, of the modern American Progressive in relation to various socio-political platforms, i.e., those with principles rooted in Socialism such as "equitable outcomes."

Surveying such arguments on Facebook, Twitter, and other social media platforms, as well as news reports from traditional media outlets or magazine articles, reveals a recurrence of several such emotional motivators in modern American Progressives: *envy, fear,* and *guilt*. This is not to say that other emotions or motivations are not present or that these affect every person leaning toward Progressive ideals. However, these three are predominately represented in common discourse and often enough in media commentary and reporting.

For example, *guilt*: Progressive-leaning individuals seem eager to announce to others that they are "guilty for the benefits that [they] receive each day." That is, they appear to feel extremely "guilty" for having been born a certain skin color or into a particular economic class. They appear miserable for the institution of slavery which they seem to consider their fault, and which demands self-hatred. They are citizens of a country that, they believe, "was founded on slavery," and that all white Americans should recognize and atone for that, including by paying reparations. *"You hated Rosa Parks for not giving up her seat,"* a social media declarant recently posted, *"and you hated Colin Kaepernick when he took a knee, and Mohamed Ali for being a conscientious objector; Shouldn't you hate yourself for slavery?"* [27]

Fear also recurred at high levels. The actual use of the word "fear," however, and unlike the use of the word "guilt," did not explicitly arise. More accurately, it was the sense of fear that could be distilled from the words used in various posts. This was especially evident when concepts such as Universal Basic Income were the topic of discussion. People who were in favor of a minimum amount of money to be paid by the government each month to everybody – at least everyone living under a certain income – expressed how more secure they would *feel*. How they could sleep better at night knowing that they would not "starve to death on the street" if they were just provided that base income each month. Others lamented that without it, they would not be able to "create art" or spend time on more important things "like family." Others believed that only with UBI would they be able to "have babies." The concept of fear as a motivator in modern Capitalist society is nothing new, but the volume of its expression on social media, including writers at major media outlets, betrays its prevalence in the emotional psychology of the Progressive.

And finally, *envy*. As will be discussed in a later chapter, it is very seldom that one will admit they are envious of someone else's success or good fortune, their wealth, status, property, or their "privilege." Envy happens to be one of the most despised emotions, and hence one that few people will admit to experiencing. Yet, words often betray true sentiments even when people try their best to hide them. Similarly, many people who are envious of other people's good fortune or the material results of their hard work, often fail to recognize that they are, in fact, envious. Either way, envy is very often disguised as a moral egalitarian concern. That is, "[e]nvious people often like to emphasize their concern for moral justice, thus attempting to justify it. Accordingly, they tend to describe their attitude as resentment rather than envy. It is clear, however, that this is a kind of rationalization of their negative attitude to being inferior." [28]

All social or political movements have opportunists and adventurers as well as fundamentalists and zealots. Whereas seeking satisfaction for one's emotions is itself not an act free of self-interest, the focus of this book is less concerned with those who clearly act out of self-interest in anticipation of increased material gain, for example, for personal or corporate profit, or for the advancement of political office or social status (e.g., those who only support a movement by pandering to its members but without sincere belief in the movement's ideology or goals). It is less concerned with uninformed voters who may tend to vote for a candidate who is promising the most "free stuff."

Rather, the primary subjects for the purposes of this book are those who either willingly, knowingly, or unwittingly have accepted the American Progressive Movement's Critical ideology or political objectives. It is concerned with those who actively or passively support the movement, including activists who promote Progressive platforms such as "Social Justice," Universal Basic Income, the Green New Deal, "The People's Budget," or Defunding the Police. Those who are, for example,

"Committed to dismantling racist, misogynist, xenophobic, and ableist institutions and systems"[29] – systems that they believe characterize all of America and all Americans. In short, those who appear to despise Americans and American life today. It also considers those Progressives who are not necessarily *activists*, i.e., who participate in furthering the Movement's goals, but who are generally aware of the Movement's ideology and believe that change is necessary in order to reach the Progressive ideal of social Utopia. Both categories of Progressives have recently begun to self-identify as being "woke" – that is, they claim to have opened their eyes and can now see America as inherently, implicitly, and systemically racist, oppressive, and "inequitable," and to such an extent that the only solution is to dismantle its institutions and culture and replace it with something different.

Along with the committed Progressive, the typical Democrat Party voter is not inconsequential. The Progressive Movement relies heavily on Democrat voters, Party support, and is always associated with Democrat Party politics. It is the modern Democrat Party that supports today's Congressional Progressive Caucus and its agenda. It is the party that appeals most to the "woke" Progressive and would-be Marxists, and the ideological division between the Party and the Movement is rapidly becoming less distinct.

In 2015, a news reporter asked the then head of the Democrat Party, Debbie Wasserman Schultz, what, if any, was the difference between the Democrat Party and Socialist Party. Wasserman Schultz was unable or perhaps unwilling to answer the question. She could only respond with a question. *"[t]he more important question is what is the difference between being a Democrat and being a Republican...The difference between a Democrat and Republican,"* she continued in answer to her own question, "*is that Democrats fight to make sure everybody has an opportunity to succeed, and the Republicans are strangled by their right-wing extremists.*"

Her response, aside from being a *red herring* fallacy, betrayed an unwillingness to admit what has become evident to those on the right of American politics: that the Democrat Party has increasingly come to adopt and promote social and political policies sounding in Progressive Socialism. It has fallen under the control of politicians, as well as the influence of pundits, who make up the American Progressive Movement. While labeling Republicans, Conservatives, and Libertarians as "right-wing extremists," the Democrat Party moves the nation further and further to one-party control and Progressive collectivist legislation that encroaches on individual rights. There is little question that the majority of the Democrat Party is falling in line with the Progressive ideology. This has been for some time evident at the Congressional level where Democrat representatives and senators consistently vote the Party-line–in "lockstep" as it were–with their party leadership, voting one hundred percent along Party-lines on major social legislation. In comparison, strict party-line voting is not the norm on the Right, and Republican Party representatives and senators are more prone to exercise individual judgment and be less influenced by an authoritarian party leadership style like that which has been on display for the last decade or so by Democrat House and Senate leaders.

Falling in line with Critical Marxist mantras, many Democrats increasingly label their own country as "systemically racist" and with "racist laws" (while often unable to cite a specific law). They admonish the Constitution for having been created by "old white men" whose main concern, they falsely claim, was slavery. While Nancy Pelosi found health insurance as a "basic human right" outlined "somewhere" in the Constitution, then Vice President Joe Biden warned black Americans that Republicans would be "putting ya'll back in chains." Emotional Democrat politicians yell "homophobe," "xenophobe," "misogynist," "racist," "white supremacist," "insensitive," and when all else fails, "micro-aggressor" at anyone who disagrees with their Progressive political position.

Democrat leaders in Congress have abandoned two and a half-centuries of legislative ethics regarding verbal *ad hominem* attacks in open debate–meant to avoid incitement to violence of the citizenry–instead resorting to almost paranoid projections on their opponents. "Get in their face!" and "[t]ell them they are unwanted!" cries Democrat Representative Maxine Waters to an emotionally charged crowd. Taking their cues from her and others, they close roads leading to a political opponent's rally, disrupt political town halls by screaming uncontrollably, weep while holding chickens to whom they have given names, and throw eggs or urine on anyone perceived not supportive of their left of center policies. Republican congressmen are assaulted by an armed assailant at an annual softball game, one critically wounded after being shot. An obviously emotionally unstable Progressive testifies at a Congressional hearing about the alleged acts of a Supreme Court Justice candidate when he was fourteen years old.

Democrat politicians consistently portray their constituents as helpless victims who would have no "opportunity to succeed" in America were it not for dependence on government. In the ultimate paradox, their calls for more freedom, more opportunity, more equality (now more equity), more choice, more "inclusion," and more "tolerance..." continually result in the promulgation of legislation meant to increase these things, but which always realizes less of them, not only for those it was designed to help but for everyone. Systematically frustrated, Progressive and Democrat policymakers actively attack the Bill of Rights, safeguards against tyranny like the Electoral College, and routinely promote giving up individual freedoms – judging them overrated in a modern society. Advocating that the 'rights of the community' as more important than individual rights, they seem to crave more government control over every aspect of an individual's existence.

Socialism, although it may have superficially morphed somewhat over the last century and a half from "class struggle" to "social justice" or "identity group struggle," is the preferred social theory for today's American Progressive Left. The hope and expectation are that the Collective – the masses as represented by a strong government–will act in everyone's best interests and the Utopian society with its pervasive "equity" will arise. Both its keystone and its Achille's heel is the "equitable" redistribution of the individual's income, earned wealth, property, or any other resource or advantage perceived by the Collective. Because Socialism's emphasis on the Collective as the ultimate moral authority–superior to the Individual–it is destructive of the individual, of his freedom, and, paradoxically, of his community and the nation. For its advocates, surrendering to a powerful, controlling authoritarian government – one seemingly necessary to maintain Collective interests and ideals – appears as a small sacrifice in comparison of the perceived psychological benefits. To understand why American Progressives prefer this subservience of the individual and the destruction of Individualism in favor of Collectivism, identifying the Progressive's underlying "psychic needs" which Collectivism appears to satisfy is imperative.

Fundamentally, the American Progressive Movement is *progress* in name only. That is, its philosophical foundation is rooted in Marxist Socialism and the naturally corrosive political states that follow. The use of the name "Progress" is today just one part of the deception that all Socialist endeavors must employ to sell what most know is an unattainable goal. This drive toward Socialism is not one that is moving forward – that is, making "progress" in human affairs – but backward. Marxism – Critical, Culture, or Scientific – is an old paradigm. Progressivism is simply a revolutionary retrograde made to look like an offensive, but with the same elusive objective to finally create the Utopian dream of a conflict-free society. However, because the name has come to describe a certain philosophy and collective of individuals who espouse it, this book will refer to it as such.

In its zeal to establish an old paradigm, Progressivism is actually taking America backward and closer to a new reality of Collectivist Fascism, Communism, and ultimately, Totalitarianism.

CHAPTER ONE

Collective Totalitarianism

"Now you can go where people are one;
Now you can go where they get things done;
What you need, my son,
Is a holiday in Cambodia"

                    - **The Dead Kennedy's, 1980**

Getting Away with Murder

B efore and during World War II, totalitarian regimes, namely Fascist Socialist Germany, Italy, and Imperial Japan were responsible for the death of an estimated twenty million civilians. Many more lives, including axis and allied soldiers were also lost in the prosecution of the War. The period during which this staggering loss of human life occurred was relatively short: between 1937 and 1945. In just the course of eight years during the Twentieth Century, the world lost nearly four percent of its population as it stood at the end of the 1930s. The Nazi efforts at genocide–the systematic extermination of more than six million Jews, Gypsies, Slavs, and other "undesirables" in concentration camps – would emerge as the defining and

1

enduring reminder of the sadistic brutality of which a people in collective submission to a state are capable. China, Korea, and the Philippines: all would bitterly remember the mass murder, rape, and torture at the hands of their Japanese occupiers well into the next century.

In the same century, however, more people were killed as the direct and proximate cause of totalitarian Socialist Communist regimes than by Socialist Fascist regimes. Marxist and Maoist Communists, since their revolutionary appearances beginning in 1917 Europe and then in post-War China, ultimately killed between eighty million and 100 million people before the end of the Century.[30] A comparable number survived extreme mental and physical torture at the hands of Communists. At the height of Communism's spread throughout the globe, a spread which became particularly virulent in the post-War period of decolonization, approximately one-third of the world's population lived under Communist rule. Between 1919 to 1989 when the Soviet Union finally collapsed in economic and cultural bankruptcy, Communist regimes had murdered or killed over four times the number of innocents than the Axis forces in World War Two had.

Failed command economic programs, like Mao's *Great Leap Forward*–a Utopian venture that caused the largest famine in history – caused an estimated thirty million Chinese to starve to death between the spring of 1959 and the end of 1961.[31] In the name of humanism and humanity, dictators like Stalin, Mao, Pol Pot, Tito, Franco, Castro, and a host of petty others sent political officers, secret police, hit squads and goons to target 'public criminals' and 'enemies of the state' – usually those who exhibited any individual human spirit or contempt for the socialist system–for extermination. Millions were summarily murdered or executed after secret or 'show' trials that provided them few rights to defend themselves. Others were sent to Gulags for 'retraining' and, if unable to be socially reformed and their individual spirit crushed, were executed, starved, or were worked to death. Although acting in the name of humanity by considering "the good of the community" or the Collective, Communist regimes "did not just commit criminal acts… they were criminal enterprises in their very essence: on principle, so to speak, they all ruled lawlessly, by violence and without regard for human life."[32] As described by the President and Fellows of Harvard University, all Socialist undertakings are criminal enterprises *ab initio.* [33] And yet, after more than seventy years since the end of World War Two and only thirty-three years since the fall of the Berlin Wall and Soviet Communism, it is Fascism that continues to be remembered as *the* political system that must, at all costs, never be allowed as a means of governance in any nation or state.

Today, accusing a political opponent, another political party, or (increasingly more common) a private person of being a "Nazi" or "Fascist" remains one of the most abhorrent insults a person can throw. It is, however, one that is cavalierly thrown about. Modern American Progressives call anyone who does not support their social and political platforms "neo-Nazis." Congressmen and women argue over which Party's members, Democrats or Republicans, are really the Nazis in an almost infantile game of "*I know you are, but what am I?*" [34] Progressive Congresswoman Ocasio-Cortez tweets,

"*Thank you @GOPLeader McCarthy for publicly confirming your desire to reward neo-Nazi members of Congress who incite violence against women under GOP leadership!*"

3

Hollywood stars like Cher make frantic, far-fetched comparisons between the U.S. Border Patrol and the Nazi secret police, the "Gestapo." Meanwhile, in a demonstration of what is arguably a mass paranoid projection, self-declared "anti-fascists" use *ad hoc* population control measures–roadblocks and checkpoints–in cities like Portland and Seattle, violently assaulting anyone suspected of being "a fascist." Many of those who loudly accuse others of being a Nazi or a Fascist appear to have little idea of what they really are. That notwithstanding, most anyone who hears these words will associate them with murder and sadism on an unprecedented scale, racial genocide, and systematic sadistic behavior. To be accused of being a Nazi is not meant as flattery.

To be called a "Communist," on the other hand, does not bring with it the same sadistic associations, even though more innocent victims were killed by Socialist Communist regimes than Fascists in the last Century. There are several reasons for this, including the sheer scale and industrial efficiency of the extermination processes that Hitler and the Nazis unleashed on the European Jews and others. [35] The Nazis, although they attempted to hide what they were doing, filmed, photographed, and otherwise kept records of their infrastructures of death. Sadistic images that were seen by the world after the War and after the suspected fate of Europe's Jews had been confirmed. Furthermore, the time span of the Nazi genocide was quite short: just seven years after it began in earnest. Whereas Communism was responsible for fourfold more deaths over the Century, it was the relative *intensity* of the Nazi perversion that placed it, and maintains it, at the top of the notoriety scale. The decisive Allied military campaign and victory against fascism also contributed to its legacy. That is, the victory was final and with firm end dates: the surrender of first Germany and then Japan. The Allied powers, almost immediately after vanquishing the Nazi army, arrested many of the general officers and others suspected of war crimes and crimes against humanity. All were put on public trial and display at Nuremberg. Their sadism and perversion were on display for the world to see in pictures, reels, and testimony. Similarly, Allied forces arrested, among others, civilian administrators and scientists involved in inhumane experiments. Many of them were convicted were hanged for their crimes.

The 1989 "fall" of Communism, on the other hand, did not result in similar treatment after the collapse of the Soviet Union and its Communist satellites. Rather, the world watched with delight and a sigh of relief as East and West Germans dismantled the Cold War's defining symbol, the Berlin Wall. Instead of focusing on the crimes committed by the Communists as they had with the Nazi generals, Western nations recognized emerging markets in the former Communist countries, and, anyway, there was no one person – like a Hitler or a Goering – upon whom they could focus blame. And anyway, the Communists did not prefer to preserve their murder and torture for history and posterity as the Germans did.

To the extent that certain (not all) of its totalitarian regimes did collapse with the dissolution of the Soviet Union in 1989, there was never any decisive "victory" that would give the democratic world the authority – nor the desire – to conduct hearings against those responsible for death and murder on numerical scales exceeding that of Nazism. Rather, the world rejoiced temporarily while watching East and West Germans integrate after more than forty years of separation, or while observing Russia presumptively transition away from a collective, centrally planned economy. There was no reckoning similar to what the world had witnessed at Nuremberg some forty years earlier. After the dissolution of 1989, some Communist dictators were brought to justice. For example, Romanian dictator Nicolae Ceausescu was taken into custody by a mob that stormed the Communist legislature and given – ironically, as he had assured others during his rule were given – a show trial, then taken out back and machine-gunned. After nearly half a century of Communist social justice, a show trial was all the people could produce. This post-Communist justice, however, was not widespread. There was no single person with command responsibility that the West, the "Free World," could prosecute and, if necessary, put to death as a deterrent and to drive home the brutality and sadistic tendencies inherent in a system that pursued with vigor the oppression of the individual, the crushing of the individual spirit, and in the name of Collectivism and the "rights of the community."

Thus, the Totalitarian perversion and mass murder inherent in Communism has been largely hidden from view. It is eclipsed by the "qualitatively" more pronounced horror of Twentieth Century Totalitarian: The *Holocaust* and its continued legacy as perpetuated and preserved in film, literature, museums, and other means that overshadow and obscure the "quantitatively" more destructive form of Totalitarianism, i.e., Communism. [36] "The Nazis," said historian and former Berkley Professor, Martin Malia, "never pretended to be virtuous. The Communists, by contrast, trumpeting their humanism, hoodwinked millions around the globe for decades, and so got away with murder on the ultimate scale." [37] Communist-era monuments glorifying those systems still stand in former Communist countries, while none created in glorification of Nazi Germany can be found.

There are few popular films, aside from a sparse collection of Cold War spy documentaries or fiction, that delve into the authoritarian, sadomasochistic nature of the societies that welcomed Socialist Communism or Fascism with their emphasis on Collectivism.

The result, at least in the Western world, is that many people have either forgotten or have never fully understood the evils of which any form of Collectivism, with its tendency toward Totalitarianism, are not only capable but inevitable.

The "Rights" of the Collective

The era of Enlightenment caused exponential propulsion of new ways of viewing the world: invention, science, mechanics, philosophy, rationalism, and the drive for efficiency in business and wealth creation (*viz.*, "to make money" – a phrase that did not exist before America's founding).[38] By the mid-1800s its effects provided the impetus for industry and mass production on a 'revolutionary' scale. Industry quickly outpaced Capitalism, particularly in the domain of unskilled labor. With factories producing like never before – providing goods at unprecedented levels to consumers at prices set by what Adam Smith called 'the invisible hand of the market–"–labor was needed in vast numbers. And vast numbers there were. In both the old country and the new (where American 'free' land for homesteading was running out and developments in agricultural science decreased the demand for farm labor) many flocked to urban industrial centers from the rural areas seeking jobs.

Whereas Smith had nearly a century before been content to write about the economic *activity* that he was seeing – activity that he correctly perceived as occurring mostly spontaneously from human nature, German-born Karl Marx was not so content. Marx had seen the effects of Europe's Industrial Revolution and the subsequent demographic shifts to urban areas with the growth and attraction of industry. As in the United States, labor was cheap and factory owners could, and often did, exploit its abundance–paying less than subsistence wages, employing child labor, demanding long hours, and with few protections for those who suffered an injury in the course of their work. The resultant growth of the urban poor and suffering was itself revolutionary. Marx set out to write an ethical-political theory with Friedrich Engels meant not only to theorize about socialism and social justice, which had been contemplated by political philosophers during previous decades but to create a plan of action to implement the theory. They published their Communist Manifesto in 1848 – a year that witnessed riots and, in several instances, bloody revolts in Germany. These revolts arose partly because of an economic depression that inhibited industrial growth during the years immediately preceding 1848, and a crop failure across Europe that led to major famine further exacerbating the condition of the poor. Although those who rioted had never read the Manifesto – it was only published that same ye–r–that would soon change.

For Marx, the true culprit that created the wretched condition of Europe's burgeoning urban poor was not industrial advancement itself. He knew the value of industry, and that efficient production was critical to improving the conditions of life for all. Rather, it was industrial progress within the framework of Capitalism, i.e., the private ownership of the means of industrial production and the resources used to fuel it. These were the tools of the oppressor: capital concentrated in the hands of the few. It was the latter's greed that caused the suffering of the masses of the poor. For Marx, Capitalism was destined to implode on its own "contradictions." Namely, those who labored, i.e., the miserable working class, would eventually be unable to afford to consume the goods they produced, and an inevitable conflict between them and the capital-and those who owned the means of production, i.e., "the rich" would ensue. This came to be called "Scientific Marxism" (which would later be criticized as taking too long to come about in the Western nations). The ultimate result, Marx concluded, would be public ownership of industry, farms, and *all* private property by the Collective. That is, the masses.

It would be the masses who owned and operated industry for the common good. They would produce it without any personal incentive or self-interest. Men would gladly surrender themselves and the products of their labor, Marx thought, for the promise of the "good life" for all. Laboring for the good of the Collective and not for themselves, people would get the basics that they needed to survive but without the ill social effects. For Marx, this was undeniably in man's best interests, so certainly he would certainly trade his true nature for not only security but Utopia – a Heaven on earth.

This Utopian concept – everyone working for the benefit of everyone else and therefore themselves – appealed to huge numbers of people experiencing or witnessing the suffering of the times. And so began a fascination with Marxist Communism that – initially the musings of a single man – became a stubborn attempt to replace man's instinctual self-interest–reflected as it was in the spontaneous rise of both economic freedom and individualism–with an artificial theory of economic sacrifice and collectivism that had never been observed in practice. [39] So appealing were Socialism and Communism on paper, that the theories were circulated widely in universities and "intellectual circles." Naturally, the thought of an attainable Heaven on earth appealed to many, not least of all the lower classes. A year after publishing the Communist Manifesto, Marx was forced to flee Prussia and seek safety in London. One story claims that Prussia sent an agent to spy on him there. Eventually, the agent made contact with Marx at the latter's apartment, where they both sat and chatted. By the time the agent left, he had grown fond of both Marx and Communism.

In 1917, however, the theory of Marxist Communism for the first time became reality in Russia. The Communist movement's leader, Vladimir Ilyich Lenin, travelled from western Europe to Russia by train where he was welcomed by his Socialist brethren – ready for dramatic social and political change in the name of equality and equity. Revolution was the word, and its work resulted in the abolition of the Russian monarchical system, the murder of the Tsar, his family, many of his loyalists, and the implementation of the Utopian ideal of collective ownership of farms and industry.

Almost immediately, Lenin and his compatriots realized that to implement the Socialist movement's Collectivist ideas, they would need to use force against those who were not buying into it. For Russian farmers, their lands were subjected to land reform and divided among the masses. Those farmers who were not particularly fond of Socialist "land reform"–freely surrendering their croplands, their produce, and the hard work that created it, to others who formed the new political collectives–were murdered. Business owners who were naturally not content to turn over their operations to those with no experience, but who were appointed to run things by decree of the collective were coerced, shamed, or "reeducated." Resistance to

Communist ideology simply was not tolerated and quickly led to murder, torture, and intense indoctrination: a combination that would continually be used over the next century to prop up the artificial collectivist mentality meant to replace human nature's chief motivator, i.e. self-interest. What Marx and his champions had failed to check for (and which the latter still fail to accept today) was the situation where one's colleague in the Collective didn't feel much like working efficiently, if at all, for his neighbors – no more than he would for an oppressive business owner. The new "humanist" ideology needed public propaganda campaigns to make them feel guilt and shame for not wanting to produce their "fair share" for the Collective. It would be a constant problem for Socialism, requiring Communist propaganda efforts up until the fall of the Soviet Union in 1989.

From the start, many doctors, lawyers, and intellectuals in the Russian brain trust who recognized the ultimate failure of the system, one that would obviously require government coercion and force to function, chose to leave Russia, leaving the Socialist Communists to themselves. [40]

As Marx made clear in his writings and theories, before a nation can create a Utopian socialist society, Capitalism must first be allowed to run its course and reach its peak. That is, a nation's infrastructure, its means of production, must be fully developed. It will then collapse on its own contradictions, after which the state will assume control over the means of production and all resources. This is Collectivism in its purest – where industry is no longer in the hands of private individuals, but "the people." Many believe that in order to reach that final stage, one more intermediate stage is necessary: a nation or society must first pass through a period of fascism, requiring first the surrender of the individual to the will of the collective, but with the means of production still in the hands of private capitalists as long as they are working toward the benefit of the collective, of the nation and the masses. Only after that stage will the Socialist elite – those academics and experts Marx assumed had the intelligence to create and direct the Utopian society – will be able to fulfill their mission of creating complete equality by completely controlling the economy along with its industry for the common welfare: "from each according to his ability, to each according to his needs."

In post-World War I Germany, however, conditions were also ripe for a new socio-political system to replace what had obviously failed. Although the Communist Manifesto had nothing at all to do with the German labor revolts and hunger riots of 1848, it did not take long for Marxist Socialist ideals to surface among Germany's Post-War destitute. After its defeat and the humiliating terms of surrender following four years of stagnant warfare, Germany was in both an economic depression and a general national malaise. As in Russia a few years before, Marxist Socialism had a powerful appeal to the German lower classes and poor. By the time of the Great Depression, more than a third of the elected German Parliament were Socialist Party members. In 1933, the leader of the German Worker's Socialist Party, Adolf Hitler – was appointed as German Chancellor.

Both Lenin and Hitler found that delivering on Socialism's promise of providing the most good for the most people (for the working masses or, in the latter case, the German nation) would require single-party political systems. Systems that would have no compunction in stripping the individual of his rights – including basic human rights – if such was deemed best for working masses or the nation. There were two systems that fit the bill: Communism as already practiced in Russia, and

Fascism. Hitler, of course, was an advocate of fascism, and as he rose to popularity, he promoted it as the ultimate political system, the one that would rally every German to sacrifice himself to combat the existential threats – internal and external – that he professed the German nation faced. Hitler remained ever ready to crush any political opposition to Fascist Socialism, including those German Communists who he persecuted as enemies of the state, later interning suspected Communists in concentration camps along with other "undesirables."

Communism and Fascism were both political systems suitable only to serve a Collectivist state and implement Socialist ideals. Fascism demanded all the nation's people to focus on and work for the interests of the nation because they were a superior race destined to rule over all others. Communism similarly demanded that all work was done for the maximum good of the working masses without emphasis on race or ethnicity, but on the ideal of classless equity. Fundamentally, however, each system required that the individual, his interests, and any rights he may have, be subservient to the interests and "rights" of the Collective, i.e., the population who made up the Fascist nation or the Communist masses; total subservience of the individual and the superiority of the governments installed to represent their respective Collectives. Fascist or Communist, the individual becomes subservient to the totalitarian state. Ultimately, he either willingly surrenders his freedom convinced by the socialist ideal in exchange for the artificial, extra-spiritual "freedom" of subservience to the Fascist or Communist Collective. [41] Or he is compelled and coerced to surrender it and comply with its demands though may they not be in his interests and are ultimately self-destructive.

"A doctrine which aims at the liberation of man evidently cannot reset on a contempt for the individual," wrote De Beauvoir, "but it can propose to him no other salvation than his subordination to the collectivity." [42] As Hegel tried to argue before Marx, for an individual to be truly free he must first submit completely to the state. This is the root oxymoron of Socialism and of the modern American Progressive ideology, that *"freedom which denies freedom."*[43] For such a false freedom to seem desirable enough to so zealously support it, it must appease some deep emotional need inside the individual American Progressive. But history shows repeatedly that Socialism does not work, and terror and violence are constantly required to resuscitate it. From Russia to Nazi Germany to modern Venezuela, Socialists required murder and terror to correct for Marx's artificial view of human nature. Men lost their individual freedom to become slaves to the Collective.

Fascism and Communism are closely related political systems – separated only by degrees. When viewed along a continuum with complete government control on the one side and complete individual freedom on the other, both Communism and Fascism require extreme interference of government into individual economic and social affairs. The political left of center is also where one associates the Democrat Party, "Liberal Democrats," Progressives, and Anarcho-Communists (those who believe in a *laissez-faire* doctrine of economics, but with complete government ownership of property).

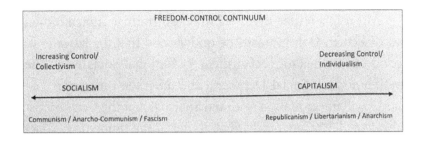

Collectivism – the social system based on the notion that the individual, his interests, his property, and his rights are subservient to the greater good of society, i.e., the Collective – is the common thread that the two systems share. The welfare of the Fascist nation or the Communist working "masses" is more important than, and superior to, any one individual. An individual's rights in a collectivist society are fewer and much more circumscribed than in an Individualist society, like that of the United States. Individual freedoms concerning speech, religion, due process, or cruel and unusual punishment, for example, were simply of no consequence if denying them to the individual was for the benefit of the collective. According to the nineteenth-century German philosopher Georg Hegel – whom both the Communists and the Fascists ideologues revered – an individual is nothing more than "a son of civil society, which has as many claims on him as he has rights in relation to it." If the collective society has rights, or "claims" as Hegel phrased it, in the individual, he or she must act only in a manner that is in the collective's best interests, not his or her own. Hegel reasoned (somehow) that the Egyptian pyramids of Giza were obviously built for the public welfare of Egyptian society, and hence those who had labored to build them were obviously obligated to do so for the public good.

Although Hitler detested the Communist International and German Communists, he understood that the latter were good candidates for recruitment as National Socialists. "The petit bourgeois Social-Democrat and the trade-union boss," he said, "will never make a National Socialist, but the Communist always will."[44] Conversely, Karl Radek – the renowned Soviet propagandist and leader of the Communist International – viewed Hitler's "Brown Shirts" (Sturmabteilungen) "as a reserve for future Communist recruits."[45] In fact, all were socialists who believed that the rights of the Collective, be it the German people or workers of the world, was more important than, and took precedence over, the rights of the individual. Whether they dedicated themselves to the nation-state as Fascists or to the world's working masses as Communists, in both Hitler's and Radek's views, was simply a matter of political cosmetics.

To Hegel, and in a paradox that consistently plagues Socialist doctrines like modern Progressivism, the individual can never truly be free unless and until he is completely subservient to the state. This means forfeiting one's natural rights for a much shorter list of rights. The freedom to speak one's contrary political or social views, for example, without fear of retaliation by the government does not exist. If the Collective deems one's speech as dangerous to the common good, contrary to government policy, or simply contrary to the public welfare, then the speaker is censored or labeled "an enemy of the State" and persecuted accordingly.

Individualism, on the other hand, is integral to those political systems that support and protect *individual freedoms*. On the Right of the control continuum, individual freedom is valued over that of government interference. Here one finds republicanism, conservativism, libertarianism, and anarchism (*laissez-faire* economics and no government ownership of property). Individualism – i.e., the socio-political doctrine that places the individual and his rights superior to that of government, can only be associated with the right of center on the control continuum. Thus Fascism (although many on the left try to project it on those right of center) can only be found on the left. That is, by its very nature, it can never take root in political systems or philosophies that value Individualism and individual freedom: laissez-faire capitalism, free-market economics, smaller government, and less government interference in personal affairs.

But individual freedom comes with individual responsibilities, personal accountability, and, most of all requires a strong sense of *self-reliance*. All these concepts can be intimidating to, and cause extreme anxiety in, those who Rousseau considered "the weak and delicate who are not suited for them." Many Progressives have a deep-seated fear of being left alone to "survive in the modern jungle." They are plagued by fears of failure or of being left to their own devices to succeed. These fears can create deep needs that are more than just animal in nature, but peculiarly human and social. The principles of Socialism seem to appeal to these hidden psychological anxieties and drive the Progressives to support Socialist political theories and policies. For many, Socialism appears as the Utopian ethical system promising the safety that one often feels in numbers – the safety of "the herd"- and the freedom from individual responsibility that comes with it.

CHAPTER TWO

Individual Freedom

"Yes! To this thought I hold with firm persistence;
The last thought of wisdom stamps it true:
He only earns his freedom and existence,
Who daily conquers them anew."

– Goethe's *Faust*

"A freedom which is interested in only denying freedom must
be denied."

– Simone de Beauvoir, The Ethics
of Ambiguity

For the last two hundred and fifty years, Americans have enjoyed and reaped the benefits of a human condition known as *Freedom*. We speak of freedom almost daily: "I can do what I want," we often hear, "it's a free country." Freedom of speech, religion, and assembly, along with a whole host of other "natural rights" are revered by mainstream Americans. They are often invoked by individuals and are protected by the Bill of Rights – a non-negotiable demand made by several of the state delegations to the Constitutional Conventions before they would ratify that founding document in 1789. Most of us *feel* we are free. We often reflect on "freedom of choice," and many of us can pick up stakes and move to another neighborhood or even another part of the country if we prefer. We can look for another job with better hours or a better wage...or not. Maryland claims it is "The Free State." Several conservative Congressional lawmakers formed a "Freedom Caucus," while even those on the political Left, e.g., the Congressional Progressive Caucus, promote their platforms and agendas by claiming they want "freedom for everyone and not just the rich." We all understand that freedom is the direct opposite of slavery, and that slavery was outlawed nationally by process of the same Constitution – for the first time in human history and less than a century after its 1789 ratification.[46]

Despite this, there is a fair share of vagueness as to what freedom really is, where it came from in its uniquely American form, or how critical it is to the human condition. Philosophers ancient and modern have attended to these questions and, as philosophers are inclined, came to no clear consensus. What *is* clear is that, while many Americans who are typically right of the political center understand and fully value freedom, there are many around us who do not. People in a modern free society are, ironically, often too busy to contemplate exactly what being free means:

"*Suddenly great old words have a hollow sound. Freedom? The average man knows in his heart what it means. His conscious concept, however, is tied up with and formulated in terms of these or those material conditions. They have been taken for granted and now they are threatened. He cannot recognize freedom, and so all meaning goes overboard and leaves a vacuum. What does 'freedom of speech,' 'pursuit of happiness,' or 'democracy' mean, unless I know how to earn a decent living by doing decent work? The scaffold of thinking that guides discourse begins to totter, confidence deserts, indefinite fear invades the bewildered mind, impairs our faculty of orientation and thus of action."* [47]

"Freedom," wrote one person recently on his social media page, "is when you don't have to worry about losing your job and going hungry, losing your health insurance, or your shelter and you can invest your energy on the things that really matter – like family, creativity, being happy, etc." [48] While emotions like worry, fear, and the search for "being happy" and "creative" are all considered part of his definition of freedom, what is obviously unclear for him is that someone else will be required to work and pay for those things he needs to find his happiness, creativity, and worry-free existence, i.e., his definition of "freedom."

To understand how emotions can undermine Freedom and how Fascism and ultimately Communism can destroy it for everyone, it's helpful to first have a deeper understanding of what freedom is in the fundamental sense and, just as importantly, how we as Americans have arrived at our current state of freedom – one that is envied by many individuals around the world who try, often employing desperate means, to come here for no other reason than to experience it and reap its benefits.

Only the human *individual* can emotionally experience freedom: to "feel free." He or she can live in, of course, a "free country," and a country may *claim* to be free, but it is only so in the sense that its people are not dominated by the forced will of another nation or that its citizens, its people, are generally not constrained by an oppressive government that prevents them from designing and pursuing their individual desires and goals. A nation, state, or collective does not experience the emotions consistent with being human – no more than any other customary or legal body, like a corporation, does. The latter may exhibit a particular corporate culture, the former a national culture, and may even be said to have a particular group or collective psyche, but as legal or theoretical constructs they do not *feel* desire, hope, happiness, or the contentment and even regret that can accompany the freedom of being able to make and pursue one's own choices in life – emotions that only individuals can experience.

Similarly, only the human individual can truly experience and appreciate the loss of freedom – having it taken from him by physical incarceration, slavery, mental coercion, or simply through intimidation and fear.[49] Although individuals may experience those emotions concomitant with a loss of freedom, the collective has no more capacity than a corporation to feel the frustration, humiliation, and the fear inherent in subservience to the state when that freedom is contested or lost.

To *be* free, an individual needs to be able to pursue her own chosen aspirations in life and to fulfill her human potential, however manifested, with which she has been graced–to be the best that she can in her choices in life and with the least amount of interference by government or any other body. A government that engages in anything more than providing those common goods necessary to pursue one's own aspirations, e.g., policing sufficient to prevent citizens from physical assault or robbery of their earnings, maintaining a professional military that protects them from those foreign powers that would aspire to impose upon them any system antithetical to freedom, and to honestly maintain the public infrastructure that provides them the opportunity to engage in private pursuits – constricts their aspirations. They are stymied and left unfulfilled in their endeavors and therefore not free. On the other hand, a government that protects one's freedom to aspire to one's fullest potential, a government that provides for those common goods necessary to pursue such aspirations, is a government whose power is checked and with the result that its citizens will experience the greatest freedom possible – for which they will willingly contribute through paying "their fair share" to support, for example, the common defense.

So where did modern freedom begin? True freedom–*the ability to chart and pursue one's course in life without interference*–was not something that appeared overnight on or around July 4th, 1776, to cause a Revolution. On the contrary, the freedom that Americans enjoy today began to take shape long ago in Europe as that continent was emerging from the Dark Ages–some seven hundred years before the American Revolution. The Dark Age (lately also called the "Gray Age" or "Dark Medieval Age") was that period in European history that followed the final destruction of the Holy Roman Empire in 476 A.D. with the defeat of Rome's final Emperor at the hands of a German Barbarian. This *coup de grace* came after a long period of Roman moral and social decline finally ending ancient Europe's glorious age – the era that saw an organized civilization of Roman law, technological advances, unprecedented feats of architectural and civil engineering, and extensive trade throughout and beyond the Roman Empire with what was then the limits of the "known world." [50]

As the continent left these "glory days" further behind, illiteracy became the norm – Latin would be lost to most, except within the Church. The Roman tradition of *chronicling* contemporary and recent history ended, leaving posterity in "the dark" as too much of what was to transpire in Europe for nearly the next six centuries. Peasants who lived during this time may have tread over stone bridges still standing or gazed upon the ruins of pillared buildings and aqueducts – still standing but dry – while having no clue as to the people who had built them, or the skills used in their creation. They had little idea of the past except what they could either immediately remember or what was passed down through storytelling. Man's creation was professed through the Church and the Bible which itself was inaccessible for most because of their illiteracy, making them dependent on the clergy to interpret it.

Europe was at this time a comparative "backwater," at least when compared to other contemporary civilizations around the world, including those in Asia and the Middle East. It engaged in little trade outside of its geographical boundaries. There was little in the way of technological invention and, in the instances that it did occur, little in the way of communicating and disseminating it outside of a small area. Invaders consistently raided and plundered: the invasions increasing in severity and frequency up through the Ninth Century. For defense, communities gathered under the protection of strong authoritarian characters – the forerunners of the Medieval period kings – who in exchange for subservience from the population, provided military leadership. Eventually, these men came to be characterized by strong autocratic rule with final and absolute authority during peacetime and supreme military command during times of conflict.

Archeologists and historians have only recently begun to learn much more about European society during the otherwise obscure period between 467 and around 1000 A.D. (hence, now often referred to as the "Gray Ages"). Vestiges of the Holy Roman Empire did certainly survive, not least of all the Catholic Church and the application of Roman law in many areas throughout the Continent. Furthermore, not all the invaders came as or remained plunderers. Many came as 'colonizers'– bringing with them their own cultural ideas and inventions. As trade gradually increased and outside threats subsided some-what, Europe boasted a rather vibrant society that moved it out of the Dark Age. What emerged around the 11th Century and the early Medieval Age was a society defined by a simple caste system: Nobility, the Clergy, and the Commoners, or "those who fought, those who prayed, and those who worked." From a per capita perspective, this system reflected a pyramid, with the nobility occupying the narrow tip, the clergy in the middle tier, and everybody else in the bottom tier.

The Nobility were the lords and landowners. They were knights and leaders who by tacit or explicit agreement offered their abilities to rally warriors, make political alliances, and lead men into battle in defense of the community or their lord. These also included the kings, a station that had been solidified during the relative anarchy and insecurity of the Dark Ages. By the time of the Medieval period, many ruled by "Divine Authority." That is, they were considered, and considered themselves, to have been ordained by God to rule over their subjects for the greater good of the kingdom. It was customary that, in exchange for the general security and welfare provided by the king, the nobles and landowners with lesser station would swear allegiance to him and rally for the defense, or offense, when called. They were all committed to the service of the king, and each in his turn could call on those able-bodied men who lived on his land to serve as foot soldiers in military campaigns. It was a necessary and willing relationship that protected both kings, nobility, the Church, and ultimately, the collective.

And the kings and their nobles had one major commodity in common: land. They were landowners of vast acreages, much of it cultivated croplands and often with huge manors or castles situated on them. In fact, by the year 1066, most European land was cultivated and owned by the nobility, with another healthy portion owned by the Catholic Church. There were, in fact, few areas not cultivated, and fewer parts were still forested. The nobles, of course, were not performing the labor needed to care for the land and make it produce. They relied upon the commoners and serfs, "those who worked." Few, if any, peasants at that time owned the land they lived on. Rather, they 'leased' it or lived on it by leave of the landowner or nobleman. In exchange, they plowed, sewed, and harvested his crops. They tended to his livestock and horses, mended walls and fences, served as woodcutters and cooks, and so forth. In short, they provided the labor that the landowner needed to maintain or increase his own wealth and status. The nobleman would also allow them to keep a portion of their harvests as sustenance for themselves and their family. Other customs included gifting something to the nobleman on his birthday, and a system of inheritance tax when the head of household died – to compensate the Nobleman for the loss of a valuable hand. Notably, there was no "wage," as we understand that word today, exchanged for the Serf's labor, but only an agreement (often hereditary and spanning generations) of subservience and allegiance to the nobleman and with the right to live on his land and benefit from his protection in return.

Children born on a noble's land were raised to learn the skills necessary to care for the noble's estate or his family.

Young boys started early at learning husbandry, repair work, planting, hunting, and harvesting. If he could acquire a weapon as a young adult, then in the event of war he could join his noble on campaign as a soldier. If lucky, he might return home with something of value looted from some conquered adversary's lands and possessions. Young women learned domestic skills and cooked for the family as well as the nobleman and his family. They made clothes and, of course, caring for the younger children. There was little opportunity except in the case of marriage, for geographical relocation. Many children born on a noble's land never left it and would later be buried on it. While he had served his own lord, his children often served his lord's sons in a continuous succession that could span generations. As with geographical mobility, there was virtually no "upward mobility" either. Largely without exception, a person lived and died as a member of the class into which he was born. The exception was for those who were accepted into the clergy – often enough commoners who swore a life of devotion at a young age to God and the Church – but also members of the nobility who forewent their inheritance for a similarly devoted life. St. Thomas Aquinas, for example, was born to a wealthy family and sent to one of the universities that were popping up throughout Europe in the new era of enlightenment. In 1243 he joined the Dominicans and lived out most of his remaining life in a Monastery.

By providing the promise of the Kingdom of Heaven upon one's death, the Church offered comfort to commoners and nobles alike. To the commoner and his terrestrial toils, sickness and disease, sorrow for the loss of loved ones, and other misfortune when it struck, his faith gave him strength, a reason to be and, when unsure, a way to look for guidance. If his life was something less than virtuous at times, the sinner was sure he could be absolved for all but the most serious of sins through confession and perhaps a fair penance. For the noble, however, if his sins were those within the more serious cardinal category, all but assuring his burning in Hell upon his death, relief was still available: through confession and absolution. Typically, this was done by a bishop or cardinal who had the power – authorization by the church–to expunge those grave sins. Of course, this cost in the way of a hefty donation to the Church, often in gold or silver but land was accepted as well. This had two effects. First and most obvious, many a noble avoided his destiny in Hell where his similarly situated serf did not. Second, the Church soon became the second-largest landholder in the Medieval world.

For the commoner, life was predetermined for him at birth. His destiny consisted of growing old and dying. Many never fulfilled that destiny, as life could be interrupted easily, early, and permanently. But despite all the hardship, life in early Medieval Europe was quite stable and secure. That is, everyone knew his place, what was expected of him or her, and what role they were to play at any given time. For the commoner, most of all, but also in some ways the nobility and the clergy, the Medieval caste system provided sociological and psychological stability. One was pretty sure to have a roof over his head each night and food on his table. Except perhaps in the most extreme of circumstances, the commoner and his family lived securely under the watch of his lord's knights and soldiers. Short of an invasion or disease, all was relatively safe.

There were few of the modern worries of society those "modern problems" such as "looking for a job," wondering where and when the next paycheck would arrive, or how to put food on the table and diapers on the children. People in those times may not yet have been free to "chart and pursue their own course in life," or to pursue fame and fortune, but for the most part they were content to live as they had always lived and generations before them had lived. If one could today ask a commoner of that time what it meant "to be free," he would likely give the inquirer a queer enough look, and perhaps his answer would suggest something like not having been taken hostage by an enemy or simply not being stuck in a dungeon somewhere. He knew his work, he had security in exchange for allegiance, and his Church promised him salvation, making his toil here on earth the more bearable.

The landowning nobility, on the other hand, were in a somewhat different position. They too had been born into their own class and with little to say about it. However, the noble not only had more control over his day-to-day affairs but also over his life-long aspirations. What allowed him this greater degree of 'freedom' was his wealth, and how much wealth, largely limited only by the volume of land he owned, was the only restriction on what he could do in practical terms of power.

Challenging Authority and the Rise of Capitalism

And power, as it has throughout the history of mankind, can corrupt. A corrupted king, such as England's King John in the 1200s, could have the desire to cause his vassals to suffer much abuse. Apparently, however, only to a point. If his vassals united against him, then he had problems. And as it happened in 1215, and in a move that is widely regarded as the first step toward the spirit of the freedom that we enjoy today, King John's vassals–his barons–did after years of abuse revolt. John had ruled over them for sixteen years by regularly employing violence, blackmail, extortion, and other abuses until his barons had finally had enough. They drafted a document, the *Magna Carta Libertatum*, that outlined restrictions on the scope of his power and that of future English kings and delivered it with an ultimatum: sign it or risk civil war and, naturally, his head.

John signed it, and in June of 1215, the Magna Carta circumscribed forever the power of English kings and provided certain "rights" for the lesser nobility. Of course, the nobles who confronted King John were not particularly concerned with the rights of their commoners, only of themselves as nobles and landholders. But as time passed and the Magna Carta endured – often invoked in English courts of Common Law – commoners began to see within its principles that they increasingly invoked for their own protection as well. It would later serve as the basis for the right to petition the courts by writ, for example, a writ of *habeas corpus* – a demand requiring an accused to be timely brought before a court and charged, and not held indefinitely without trial. It also became the source of more legal protections and principles that would not only find their way into England's courts, but also in the country's future colonies and directly into the United States Constitution and Bill of Rights (including the Fourteenth Amendment, passed after the American Civil War, whose provisions can be traced directly back to the Magna Carta).

Still, for the commoner in the immediate aftermath of the events of 1215, not much was different in the way of freedom. This began to change in the middle of the Fourteenth Century. The agent of that change was the Bubonic Plague, also known as the *Black Plague* or, as it was known in Europe during its time, simply the *Black Death*. By the 1300s, Europe was no longer a 'backwater' with little international trade. Cities and seaports of significant size had developed, many boasting growing artisan classes and facilitating robust trade with cities in North Africa and the Middle East. Along with the sea trade in goods, of course, came the animal kingdom's natural stowaway: the black rat. He brought with it a flea that brought with *it* the Black Plague bacteria.

The Plague had been running its course in China, India, Persia, and Egypt before finally making its way along trade routes to Europe in 1347. In the course of a few short years, the Plague hit all parts of Europe, and although it would come back time and again to cause new outbreaks in Europe during the next one hundred years, this first outbreak devasted Europe's population. In some cases, the populations of entire towns were wiped out. Histories document young children that were found alone – living quite ferally – after their entire family and community had succumbed to the plague. People diagnosed with the plague in the morning were often dead by evening – if they were lucky. Others, depending on the method of infection, wasted away more slowly and in great pain before succumbing. Within just a decade, the Plague took with it upwards of fifty percent of Europe's continental population.

This death rate dramatically affected the economic relationship of the commoner with the noble. As the Plague took its toll, the workers – on whose labor the nobles depended to make their lands profitable – began to be buried in it instead of working on it. In many instances, whole communities disappeared as the Black Death took all inhabitants with it, leaving no one to take care of the noble's lands. In other cases, it was the nobles themselves – often enough along with their extended families–who passed into eternity. The net result was vast tracts of lands and outbuildings deserted, unclaimed, and as the plagued years wore on, overgrown. For the first time in history, there was a labor shortage, and it was this shortage that signaled the ushering in of the vestiges of a new phenomenon – Capitalism.

Labor – or its scarcity – became in the mid-1300s western Capitalism's most resonant commodity crisis. Commoners used it to barter with desperate nobles who needed it. Better working conditions and in some cases, remuneration besides just the usual "room and board" were the result. For the first time, commoners began working for and expecting a wage. If one landowner couldn't or wouldn't pay a wage, or a high enough wage, then a commoner might find a better wage from the next landowner down the pike. Likewise, commoners and their families could simply pick up stakes and occupy lands that were now deserted due to the Black Death having done its work not only on the noble landowner but all his legal heirs. After clearing it, caring for it, and then making it produce for decades, commoners quieted these lands as their own. In that way, once serfs, they now began creating their own wealth, self-reliance, and new social status.

Meanwhile, trade with distant lands resumed and as the economy again took off, a burgeoning merchant class began to develop – "new money" dynasties began to arise with demand for imported goods from distant lands, and distant demand for exported European goods increased. The discovery of the Americas in 1492 created demand for Caribbean products such as sugar and coffee (and setting off what would come to be called "the Colombian Exchange"). Whereas Columbus had been required to rely upon Queen Isabella to finance his initial voyages in search of a shorter trade route to India, as exploration of the Americas continued, groups of investors began to pool their own money and share the risks of financing ventures across the Atlantic for profit – to "make money" as it were for profit's sake – and not so much for *gloria patria*. Mercantilism – the economic theory of the day – was being upended by Capitalism and its growing "middle" and "upper middle" classes. It was the making of money for the benefit of the investor, the artisan, and the laborer according to his strengths; and the western world would soon see it level the power of 'divine authority' with a rapid pace.

Individualism – Economic Freedom's Natural Companion

Just a few years later, in 1505, a young man named Martin Luther gave up on a very short career studying law to join the Order of the Hermits of St. Augustine. Luther was to pursue his Christian faith passionately, openly challenging Rome on several of the strongest tenets of the Catholic Church – the single Western religion as Europe stood in the early 1500s. Luther was so outspoken in his arguments with Rome that warrants for his arrest – and the burning of his anti-Catholic writings – were routinely ordered by Papal decree. Ultimately, Luther's writings and polemics would serve as the catalyst for the Reformation – the religious protest and upheaval that caused the Church to split between Catholic and Protestant. Luther's focus would both conflict with and follow Christ's notion of personal responsibility, i.e., that the Kingdom of Heaven awaited those who did God's work here on earth. That is, Luther believed that Christ's sacrifice was atonement for original sin and that one's entrance to Heaven could be attained through faith alone, and not necessarily "earned" as Catholicism professed.

For Luther, Christians were predestined to enter Heaven – and this ultimately militated against the individual's dependence on the Church. The individual was a free agent who did not need the Church to determine – most controversially through the purchase of a letter of indulgence ridding one of their sins – whether he should be allowed salvation and entrance to God's Kingdom upon his death. Luther's Reformist views were adopted by Calvin – a second-generation Reformist. Calvin further professed a belief that God's extension of salvation to "sinful" humanity was an enigma, emphasizing that Hell was still an option. Consequently, Reformists began to have some doubt about how exactly God wanted them to act while on earth. The solution for Protestants was to maintain a strict spiritual focus in one's daily life on *work*: an unceasing commitment to one's "calling" or vocation in life.[51] What developed was a strict "Protestant work ethic" that was heretofore unseen, or at least unknown, in history. It was an individual industriousness that has been described as a vigorous *willingness* to labor of which no pharaoh or king could ever conceive. Furthermore, frugality and asceticism in enjoying or spending the fruits of one's labor was also essential to maintain Godliness. According to sociologist Max Weber, this combination of work ethic and conservation of earnings resulted in a rapid accumulation of capital.[52]

And it would primarily be Protestants, adherents to both Luther's and Calvin's Reformist theology, who would initially settle in the northern American continent. They would bring with them the spirit of work, individualism, spiritual freedom, and the spirit of self-reliance with which the still developing phenomenon of Capitalism would symbiotically thrive in America. [53] Thus, by the mid-1600s, North America boasted several strong colonies that had been founded and settled by those religious dissidents. Although there was a growing spirit of individualism and independence among the colonists, England was content to leave them alone: to ultimately let them administer their colonies and determine their legislatures, religious institutions, and militias how they saw fit. And the colonists eventually thrived – producing indigenous crops like tobacco and corn as markets and demand developed for them in England and continental Europe, as well as natural resources and refined products like timber that England needed for shipbuilding. With successive generations being born with identities more "American" than British, the rift between the old and new worlds grew. Life in America was in all respects a challenge, one not for the faint of heart, and on its shores grew a unique character that was extremely self-reliant, steeped in faith, and ruggedly individualistic. Not least of all, he was self-interested and increasingly wary of government regulation and misappropriation.

Once England and the Crown realized how productive these new "Americans" were – competing with England's economy in both size and activity – it began to demand its 'fair share' in taxes, eventually sanctioning monopolies in trade and passing several acts, like the Stamp Act, that would ensure tribute to the Crown. And so, amid cries for "liberty" and "freedom," the lid blew off in July 1776, leaving in its wake the first government uniquely "of the people for the people," and with the people's individual, natural rights explicitly protected from infringement by virtue of their Constitution. Such was the power of this new spirit of freedom that immediately after the ratification of the Constitution in 1789, many of the new states – and for the first time in human history–outlawed slavery as contrary to their own similarly crafted state constitutions. Pennsylvania's legislature did not even wait for a Constitutional convention. Its colonial legislature outlawed slavery through a process beginning in 1778 - only two years into the Revolutionary War. Within eighty years slavery would be outlawed federally by virtue of the federal Constitution and after a war that almost permanently destroyed the union.

Hence, it was principles of Capitalism that had brought feudal society in Europe to an end by providing a means of upward mobility for the legacy commoners to earn wages – individuals who could earn and dispose of their wealth, large or meager, how they saw fit. Europeans paid to send their children to be educated in the new universities that were cropping up in early Medieval centers in Italy, Germany, the Netherlands, and England. Others invested in export-import and ancillary activities in a growing world economy. Others risked parts of the accumulated wealth in speculation and venture-style risk-taking. These opportunities were soon on par with land ownership as a means to achieving wealth and, with wealth, the freedom to transcend one's station in birth and in life. It was Capitalism that allowed a laborer the freedom to seek a better wage elsewhere. The value of work and the notion of collecting wealth – i.e., money – commensurate with its value, allowed men to control more and more aspects of their own lives without reliance upon a monopolistic, landowning nobility. Europe was unwittingly creating a unique avenue to a level of freedom not achieved before in human history. This was Capitalism and it was leading men increasingly, albeit sometimes painfully slow, to individual economic freedom.

Capitalism made man free, even if just a little by giving him an edge over what would otherwise be a predetermined destiny in the old Feudal system. It was the natural companion of Individualism: both nourished each other as men acquired a little or a lot of wealth and could therefore write their own paragraph or their own chapter in life. "Economic freedom," wrote Fromm,

"Was the basis of this development, the middle class was its champion. The individual was no longer bound by a fixed social system, based on tradition and with a comparatively small margin for personal advancement beyond the rational limits. He was allowed and expected to succeed in personal economic gains as far as his diligence, intelligence, courage, thrift or luck would lead him... in the feudal system the limits of his life expansion had been laid out before he was born; but under the capitalistic system the individual, particularly the member of the middle class, had a chance – in spite of many limitations – to succeed on the basis of his own merits and actions." [54]

Europeans – and after 1776, Americans in particular–were more in control of their lot in life than ever before in the history of mankind. Capitalism's benefit was to the individual, giving him (and ultimately, her) the maximum amount of freedom in making economic decisions with the money that they earned and therefore more freedom to chart their course in life. Economic freedom is inextricably intertwined with, and a necessary condition of, individual freedom

CHAPTER THREE

Human Political Psychology

"When I took a decision or adopted an alternative, it was after studying every relevant – and many an irrelevant – factor. Geography, tribal structure, religion, social customs, language, appetites, standards – all were at my finger-ends. The enemy I knew almost like my own side."

– T.E. Lawrence ("Lawrence of Arabia"), 1919

Natural Selection, Emotion, and Survival

Sociology has been the lens through which group political or social behavior has been traditionally viewed by analysts. However, because social and political groups are made up of individuals who share common interests – certain worldviews, political or social philosophies, or common objectives–many other disciplines become relevant. Increasingly, these have been applied at their intersections to the analysis of political behavior. For example, law, history, anthropology, economics (particularly the influence of "self-interest" in determining economic behavior), religion, moral philosophy, ethics, and not least of all, the psychology of human emotion. Even the "hard sciences" of human chemistry and biology, including genetics and the principles of natural selection, have become relevant as scientists have uncovered the physical processes involved in emotional behaviors. All have increasingly been integrated into attempts to analyze individual and group political behavior.

Human emotion is a peculiar phenomenon, even in just the wide range of emotions of which we are capable and for which we don't need "training." A two-year-old will hang his head in *shame* in front of his mother when he has done something that they both understand he probably should not have. [55] Conversely, he will beam with *pride* and smile when he's done something praiseworthy – perhaps learned to buckle himself into his highchair for the first time. He feels *happy* about it. When her primary caregiver disappears for a period a toddler may experience *anxiety*, or if there is an adult stranger in the house she may cling in mild *fear* or apprehension to her parent's leg. She may do something that obviously harms another person – causing her to feel the very uncomfortable emotion of *guilt*. As a boy matures, he realizes by degrees that other people (yes, including even girls) have feelings too. Hopefully, he develops a keen sense of empathy. Starting with his immediate family, he may develop those feelings of attachment that we typically associate with *love*: first for his family, then maybe for someone outside of his family, and later – arguably the greatest love of all – love for his own children.

It is not possible for a person to "teach" someone else how these emotions *feel*. Nobody taught the child *how* to feel shame, pride, jealousy, or how guilt and even love should feel. We are already hardwired–biochemically – and the chemical reactions that cause emotions are simply waiting for the right environmental circumstances to activate them, sending those feelings, those "waves of emotion," through the brain. Even if temporarily, emotions can cause us to act or react in ways that are productive and at other times destructive.

Contemplation of human behavioral psychology, however, has been around a long time: at least two thousand years before the advent of modern psychology, Freudian psychoanalysis, and newer psychoanalytical paradigms. In ancient times, men commonly blamed the trickery of the gods when trying to understand and explain human emotional states like anger, love, hate, and jealousy. They developed folklore, fables, and myths describing the power of these emotions, for better or worse. Modern psychology often borrows many terms from, for example, Greek mythology, including *Psyche* herself: the Greek goddess of the soul who was targeted by other goddesses envious of her beauty and the admiration that people bestowed upon her.

Ancient philosophy, including political philosophy, was arguably a forerunner of modern psychology. Those philosophers collectively known as the Stoics, for example, as early as the ancient Greek and Roman eras, had attempted to identify not only the nature of man's various emotions, like envy, anger, and fear but how one could control them and not be controlled *by* them:

"I will conduct you to peace of mind by another route: if you would put off all worry, assume that what you fear may happen will certainly happen. Whatever the evil may be, measure it in your own mind, and estimate the amount of your fear. You will soon understand that what your fear is either not great or not of long duration." [56]

After the dawn of the European Enlightenment, philosophy began again to wrestle with questions of human behavior, including the nature of political power. The desires of men or "man in his natural state" were the baseline for many Enlightenment philosophers like Hobbes, Rousseau, and others. Ultimately, they focused on the nature of the rights of man in relation to their ruler: the king and, later, non-monarchical government. In Western culture, notions of democracy, liberalism, and republicanism–after having been dormant since the Golden Age of Greece -became relevant topics of enlightened contemplation and, ultimately through social upheaval, practice. As these philosophical ideas developed (and with the invention of the printing press were disseminated on an increasingly unprecedented scale) freedom from tyranny and positive, individual freedom was increasingly understood as the ideal human state. The philosophy of ethics developed, contemplating what people should or should not do in a particular conundrum involving human relations, *viz:* deciding what is the morally right thing to do in relation to the welfare of others. Concepts such as "fairness" (later developing into "fair play") became part of the knights' Code of Chivalry: their morals on how they should conduct themselves personally and in relation to others, not least of all other knights, ladies, and children.

Although ethical behavior varies among cultures, every human society develops a certain set of behaviors to which it expects its members to conform and with the conscious or unconscious realization that doing so keeps the society from disintegrating. It forms the so-called "moral fabric that holds a society together." Ethical dilemmas arise, however, when fact patterns are outside the norm or more complicated; when determiningwhat really *is* the "morally right" thing to do is not so clear. Organized politics is arguably the one human activity that creates more major ethical dilemmas than any other. And no other organism in the Animal Kingdom practices politics: not the pack, not the den nor the herd.

Animal struggles for dominance – whether in the pack or the pride–are manifested by physical posturing or violence to some degree. These physical manifestations are motivated by the survival instinct: biological urges genetically ingrained through natural selection promote the animal's survival at least long enough to procreate and thereby help ensure the survival of the species. The dominant specimen is the one that procreates, thus not only ensuring the survival of the species generally but of the dominant (i.e., fittest) specimen (Darwin's "survival of the fittest").

Natural selection determines which offspring, usually in combination with a genetic mutation and a rapid or radical environmental change, are better equipped to survive. Those who did survive long enough went on to reproduce, promulgating their unique inherited genetic traits that favored survival. For a popular example, opposing thumbs: likely a mutation that allowed humans to grip more powerfully and to have better control of objects like stone tools or smartphones; or the small toe that might look passively useless, but necessary for our ability to walk upright on two feet. The ability to walk upright provided a better chance to survive through a higher perspective to view either prey and predator, color eyesight to distinguish and identify what surrounds us, and the other senses of smell, and taste (e.g., to help distinguish harmful or poisonous plants), touch and hearing.

Human psychology, specifically including our emotional makeup, is also part of our evolutionary process and human emotions have similarly been linked to the survival instinct and natural selection.[57] A result of natural selection, emotions serve some purpose related to survival, just as the physical manifestations of human evolution have. Those humans who were the first to be inhibited with the chance chemical processes to *feel* emotionally were, in response to some outside or environmental stimulus, likely more able to survive and thus more likely to live long enough to procreate. For example, the *fear* emotion has obvious roots in the survival mechanism. It can cause a chemical release of adrenaline meant to prepare the body for increased performance in the "fight or flight" reaction. The inability to fear one's predators could – obviously–have absolute consequences on the ability to be around long enough to procreate. Along the same lines, those in the evolutionary process in which fear was not present were likely to succumb before having an opportunity to pass on those emotional processes to future generations.

However, the evolution of human emotion was not limited to survival in the face of immediate physical threats that, for example, the fear emotion, helped overcome. Social interaction and the potential for human association to protect the survival of the individual and thus guarantee the propagation of the species was also a response to psychological evolution. Many emotions, including love, jealousy, envy, shame, and pride are relative to other human beings (the *objects* of our emotions). They assist in navigating through human relations and affairs. In short, human-specific psychology is "a diverse array of neurocomputational programs that were built by *natural selection* and are functionally specialized for solving ancestrally recurrent adaptive programs." [58]

The ability to feel the *love* emotion was probably with the objective of securing the extended association of one's mate (or in a broader sense one's friends or 'significant others'). This may have kept biological parents, for example, together longer and thus in a better position of physical security while the newborn (which one also came to *love*) required care. The family unit thus provided better security, shelter, and food for the young and the nursing mother. Perhaps the *jealously* emotion – guarding the object of that valued love relationship from interference by a perceived challenger – may have followed the evolution of the *love* emotion. Empathy, the ability to sense the emotional state present in others, gave rise to morals and ethics.

Taking it a step further, modern social scientists have contemplated the c*oncept of human political psychology*: the study of how emotions affect people's political decision-making. It explores both the superficial and the deeper psychological needs of the individual, those needs that can and often do influence a person's support for one political or social doctrine over another, or one candidate over another. Many consider human political psychology as inherited through the same or similar biological evolutionary processes as natural selection. Survival is survival, and sometimes changing political and social interactions and allegiances can make all the difference. As a type of survival instinct, some humans acquired the capacity to adapt to, or when necessary, change political and social interactions that were required for the survival of the individual, e.g., the formation of the family unit or for the survival of the larger group, the herd. As humans developed, this ultimately came to include "communal" concepts such as the redistribution of resources among the members of the group, like the meat from a large animal hunt. Such cooperation kept all nourished and thus contributed to the survival of the group and therefore higher protection of all from outside threats. In short, the community was stronger when it cooperated on any level, and the well-being of the individuals that made up the community was that much higher and more secure.

This is consistent with the theory that "[t]he human mind has been organized by natural selection to respond to evolutionarily recurrent challenges and opportunities that pertain to...social interactions." [59] Human social interaction developed from individual to family and to community. "Man in his state of nature" – that favorite starting point for political philosophers since the Renaissance - is beyond the scope of this book. However, the evolution of emotions that helped create *social man* by helping him recognize, for example, that he was stronger and more secure from existential threats when in the company and companionship of others like him, likely created a psychology affecting *social policy*. At some point there developed a requirement for the group to work cooperatively, or at least not hostile toward each other, to survive. This included sharing or "redistribution" of resources within the group.

And it is the redistribution of resources that underlies *all* modern political activity – who gets to say what resources need to be shared and how we're going to share them (or in modern terms, how much and who are we going to tax and how are we going to spend the money). With a little speculative help from Rousseau and modern anthropological studies, we can safely assume that this "politicking" has been going on since about the time a man and woman decided to stick together with their offspring, or even with the latter's offspring in an extended, intergenerational family. Politicking likely intensified after a few families decided to stick together for the common good, and group decision-making likely from the start resulted in disagreements that required some consensus to resolve.

The role that emotion plays in an individual's social and political choices is often underestimated or, perhaps more accurately, underreported since most do not like to consider that emotion is driving their political choices. Yet, many people do make political choices and support social platforms based on their emotions.

As Clemenceau famously remarked in the 19th Century, "Not to be a socialist at twenty is proof of want of heart; to be one at thirty is proof of want of head."[60] "Bleeding heart Liberal" is an often-used pejorative meant to describe those on the political left who are affected by this phenomenon. As Liberals are philosophically akin to, if not now synonymous with, Progressives, the term is appropriately applied to the latter. And thinking with one's "heart" is, of course, appealing to one's emotion. Allowing emotion to drive one's political choices necessarily comes at the expense of logic and informed reasoning, to wit: "want of head."

And there are many emotions that can influence one's personal, political, and social decision-making: pity, fear, guilt, envy, jealousy, pride, selfishness, compassion, sadness, and joy to name just a few. Our vast array of possible emotions makes us human, and we all experience their effects daily. Some are pleasing, like pride and joy. Others, like envy or jealousy, not so much so. The latter type can evoke very uncomfortable feelings and anxiety, compelling us to act in ways that we shouldn't. Sometimes the emotions persist longer than we would like them to, for example when we experience guilt for having caused someone else harm.

Several particularly powerful human emotions can be associated with the American Progressive's political psychology, including *envy*, *fear*, and *guilt* (essentially, the faux "guilt" that is often associated with Progressive theories like Critical Race and other post-modern or non-positivist theories). As with many emotions, these can be sources of anxiety, sadness, depression, and even self-hate, for example, believing oneself to be a citizen of a country allegedly founded on racism and systemically racist. If left unmitigated, the uncomfortable and even painful feelings they produce can become all-consuming and debilitating–severely affecting one's enjoyment and personal satisfaction in life itself. If chronic, they can lead to not only irrational decisions but also self-defeating and destructive behavior.

Economic Freedom's Emotional Companions

It is no coincidence that as European Feudalist society began to disintegrate with the spontaneous rise of economic freedom and Individualism – when serfs and commoners acquired a certain level of self-reliance and independence from the nobility – those certain emotions increasingly became evident. For example, as some participating in the increasingly free market system came to acquire more wealth than their neighbors, moral considerations and discussions regarding the emotion of envy increased proportionally. The first indicator of this was in the Christian sacrament of Confession or Penance. Penance was introduced by the Church as compulsory in the Thirteenth Century. A penitent would confess his sins to a Confessor, typically a priest or bishop, and in response would be absolved of them. For Church moralists–those who served as the sole providers and guides for moral interpretation in European society – penance (a/k/a "confession") began to reveal what appeared to be an increase in penitents coveting what their neighbor or some acquaintance had, i.e., of being envious. They were neither sure why the increase, nor were they even sure what envy was. They often confused envy, like modern people often do, with jealousy. Either way, "Thou Shalt Not Covet Thy Neighbor's Goods" was one of the Ten Commandments, and it seemed to comport with what the Church was seeing increasingly on the ground via the practice of penance and in the confessions of the repentant. To help clarify and accurately assess the frequency of feelings of envy in penitents, in 1216 the Church required that its Confessors "inquire of the penitent if he grieves or has grieved over the advantages of his neighbor, or if he has been glad of his neighbor's misfortune." Although the Church had yet to identify these feelings as envious, they were since "grieving" over another's advantage is indicative of the emotions, as is the ancillary emotion of taking delight in the envied other's misfortune (what psychoanalysts call *Schadenfreude*).

The increase in the envy emotion throughout Medieval society that the Church had originally identified has been substantiated by historical scholars. Beginning with controlled surveys of Twelfth and Thirteen Century European literature, including novels, poetry, satire, and chronicles, researchers have found few occurrences of the word "envy." One version of *Lancelot du Lac* had the most occurrences of a single text produced during this time: six. [61] Surveying Fifteen Century literature – after European trade had increased significantly and the growing wealth among and between commoners was challenging and competing with the wealth of the traditional nobility–"the frequency of the word 'envy' explodes" in literature, chronicling, and in the new emphasis on the study and contemplation of philosophy that emerged in the early Renaissance period (1400-1500). [62] It is also during this period that envy becomes associated with feelings of hatred and a desire for power. "The desire for power," wrote Jean Delumeau, "did in fact lead to implacable hostilities, among them the Great Schism of the West [of the Roman Catholic Church between 1378 to 1417], the French and English civil wars, and the rivalry between the dukes of Burgundy and the kings of France. Men turn out to be each other's Cains. Envy – as Aquinas noted – is worse than death." [63]

As economic freedom and Individualism advanced on their natural course, commoners who before were serfs with little or no wealth of their own, living communally as it were on a noble's land and all equally under a noble's charity, soon began to see differences in wealth among themselves. Although, and is commonly seen even today, commoners were not particularly envious of those in classes much more distant than their own, viz., the nobility class. However, the same was not true regarding their neighbors who had risen to an economic class much nearer to their own. This was particularly acute as parvenus began to show off their new wealth and status in the manner of their dress, wealth and status: in the manner of their dress, their newly acquired "refined" social habits, their acquisition of domestic servants, and other public displays or indicators of their upward mobility.

Envy, it seems, was one of several unanticipated emotional companions of the new economic and individual freedom emerging within an ever increasingly free-market culture – one that was leaving the relative social stability of Feudalism behind.

CHAPTER FOUR

Envy

"There be none of the affections which have been noted to fascinate or bewitch, but love and envy."

– **Francis Bacon, c. 1625**

"All History is class-war; all Life is class-war; they have the wealth, let us take it."

– Francis Yockey, Imperium, 1948

T he perils of envy have been the subject of parables, stories, and fables for time immemorial. In folklore, fable, myths, and movies, humans have for thousands of years tried to warn posterity about its destructive potential. Stories dating back to ancient Rome and Greece tell of horrible deeds done by envious neighbors, brothers and sisters, kings, and even envious peoples and cities against other groups or cities. The envious person sees that someone else possesses something that he would like to have but which he perceives is unattainable: more wealth, a particular lover, or even a higher degree of popularity. In many of these stories, the envier comes to despise the envied person and either attempts to harm him in some way or, failing that, to destroy and deprive him of the thing that the envier so desires. Often, this comes at the cost of the envier injuring or even destroying himself in the process.

In the Bible, Cain becomes envious of his brother, Abel, who – Cain perceives – has received undeserved favor from God. Frustrated and considering it unjust that he himself could not attain the same level of favor from God as did Abel, Cain kills Abel. Cain's evil deed is found out, and he is banished forever as a wanderer. Through the Ten Commandments, God instructs that "[t]hou shalt not covet they neighbor's house…ox or donkey….wife…or anything that belongs to your neighbor."

The Greek hero Ajax, one of the warriors who had fought aside Achilles at Troy, became the object of envy by the men of Athens. They envied his reputation as a skilled warrior second only to the renowned Achilles. After Achilles' death, they influenced a contest between Odysseus and Ajax that would decide which of them would receive Achilles' coveted armor. As a result, Odysseus was declared the winner, and Ajax, himself hopelessly envious of Odysseus' new possession, later flies into a blind rage killing what he, in his madness, thought was Odysseus and the men of Athens. Turns out, it was just a bunch of helpless farm animals. After coming to his senses and seeing what he had done, he took his own life out of disgrace.

In his fables, Aesop told of a dog carrying a bone in his mouth. When he walks by a pond, he sees his own reflection in the water. Perceiving the reflection to be another dog with what looks like a more desirable bone than he himself has, he opens his jaws as he lunges for the bone in the reflection, dropping and losing the only true bone into the deep. A more modern story found in different cultures tells of an envious man who is granted one wish from a goddess (or a "genie" depending on which version). The man is elated at first, but then the goddess informs him that, whatever riches he may receive, the goddess will bestow upon the man's neighbor twice as much. The thought of his neighbor possessing twice as much of something than he compels the envious man to think hard for a while before choosing. He then asks the goddess to poke out one of his eyes.

Envy, however, does not exist only in folklore and fable. Rather, it is a very real human emotion whose effects can at times be debilitating. Envy is a desire to possess some tangible or intangible thing that another person, someone whom the envier often perceives as superior, possesses. [64] The envier looks at another's nice house, of the better neighborhood in which the other lives. Perhaps another's superior talent, for example in music writing, is the thing envied, or the other's popularity or influence. It could be a higher level of personal "virtue" that the other is able to signal to an audience, a level that the envier believes is a more socially desirous level that he should have for himself – a condition that often results in attempts to publicly "virtue signal" at a higher intensity than one's competitor.

Although most people are able to manage their envious feelings, some cannot. The envier's thought that she lacks another's desirous possession, her superior qualities or achievements is for her "a significant threat to self-esteem." [65] She views herself as inferior in some way to the person she envies, and this feeling may persist to the point that the envier is and remains miserable. "Envy is so uncomfortable, in fact, that it has been linked to the activation of neural circuitry that is responsible for physical pain." [66]

But there are some conditions before such pain and threats of loss of self-esteem arise. First, only when it is impossible for the envier to attain the thing that he considers so desirous, and which the envied person has, can the envy emotion form. That is, there must be a *gap*: one that the envier cannot bridge by, for example, simply going out and getting the same desirous thing for himself. The necessary gap need not be real. The envier only needs to *perceive* that a gap exists, only that he *believes* that he can never have what the envied person has even though that may not be true. And the envied person herself may not even possess the thing that the envied person sees as so desirous. It is sufficient, for example, that the envier believes that the envied person has a certain desirable influence, popularity, or some other quality, even though that really isn't' the case. In his poem, *The Vision of Hell*, De Quevedo tells of several envious persons who, upon their arrival to the depths of Hell and seeing the torture and pain inflicted on the souls that preceded them, became immediately envious because they felt that there would be none left for themselves. [67] Here, the envied object itself is nothing that a rationally thinking person would ever consider desirable.

Second, even when a gap is real it is still possible that the envy emotion does not arise. If the desirable thing is possessed by someone in a social or economic class that is more distant, usually much higher than the class in which the envier sees himself, the envy emotion is less likely to form. For example, a businessperson who earns a "middle-class income" is not likely to be envious of, say, a Jeff Bezos or an Elon Musk. They are entrepreneurs in quite another league than the middle-class businessperson. Instead, it is those who are closest in economic or social status to the envier that typically become the target of their envy. The middle-class businessperson, to the extent that she is prone to envy, is more likely to become envious of another person who is closer to her as an economic peer – a person who is doing much better financially than she is, but not excessively so that she is several income classes removed.

Similarly, a Bezos could become envious of a Musk or a Zuckerberg, as one's fame and reputation for accomplishment – if considered desirable–begin to outpace the other (not saying they are). An established Hollywood star is more likely to be envious of another star whose popularity, acting skills, or public demonstrations of "social virtue" are only just superior to her own. An otherwise unknown, aspiring actress, on the other hand, is not likely to be truly envious of either of the two established actresses. It is only when the other person is someone close in status, whether a fellow pauper or a king's contemporary, that true envy arises. In this case, the envied person is sometimes referred to as the "similar other" as he or she is comparatively closer to the envier in respect to the gap that separates them from the unattainable envied thing or quality.

Envy should not be confused with other feelings that outwardly may *appear* as envy but really aren't. For example, if seeing your neighbor driving the latest model hybrid automobile causes you to go to the dealership, trade-in your old car, and buy the same eco-friendly model as your neighbor, then perhaps you're not really trying to "keep up with the Jones." You're not truly envious because you have the means to buy that hybrid car too, and in fact you did. You were able to "close the gap." Or maybe you chose *not* to buy the same automobile, but the option was still there and hence there was no real or even perceived gap between you and your neighbor. Also, people often expressly use the word 'envy' in a more lighthearted manner (most truly envious people avoid even using the word to describe their feeling since such would be an admission to what is considered one of the more odious emotions). For example, telling a friend or colleague that you "envy" their ability to act calmly in times of stress, or that you envy them for taking the time to pay attention to the more important things in life, like family and political contemplation. Or you admire their decisiveness, persistence, or some other good quality. You don't truly envy them in the emotional sense. Rather, you are sort of complementing them. You are outwardly recognizing them for that admirable quality that they have and you're saying–in a friendly way–that you too should probably strive a little harder to enjoy that quality as well.

True envy is a natural emotion, and everyone has an episode with it from time to time. This *episodic envy* is the quantitative form of envy that is simply natural, just part of our human wiring. Those who may have once been envious of another's good fortune, or perhaps enjoyed a little too much in someone else's "bad karma" (i.e. *schadenfreude*) after an envied person was visited by misfortune, are simply feeling episodic envy that may arise infrequently and then subside without much fanfare. After having experienced an envious episode once or twice in life as they mature, most people recognize it for what it's worth and are better able to toss it aside, so to speak, or mitigate its effects in the future. *Dispositional envy*, on the other hand, is something more pronounced and consistent in a person's personality. He is constantly on the lookout for who has something more than him, what it is, and how much better off the envied person is for having it. Unfortunately, it may not stop there. Such strong feelings of envy can affect one's mental health – that loss of self-esteem and the feeling of almost physical pain–to the point where he or she is sullen, depressed, and life is anything but enjoyable.

Malicious Envy

Whereas episodic and dispositional envy describe a quantitative measure (i.e., either occasional or chronic), there are two broad, qualitative measures of envy: *malicious* and *benign*. They are categorized mainly by how the envied person reacts to feelings of envy. That is, how a person deals with his or her envious emotions. The first, *malicious envy*, is the destructive variety. The one with which we are all familiar in the folklore and fable that warns us of its destructive tendencies. [68] When an envious person begins to harbor true feelings of ill-will or malice toward the envied person, antisocial behavior can result. At worst, this can include subversion, retaliation, infliction of psychological distress, or even physical violence against the envied person. It can also conjure up a desire to destroy the coveted or desired thing with the intent to deprive the envied person of the thing's enjoyment. "If I can't have it," says the malicious envier, "neither shall she." At best, depression, feelings of low self-worth or self-esteem, and even self-effacing, self-destructive, and masochistic behavior can result.[69] Overall, "people who are inclined to experience malicious envy make fewer positive impressions on others, undermine superior's successes with aggressive strategies, and, ultimately, reach worse wellbeing." [70]

Malicious envy can consume an individual's thoughts. When it is present to such a degree that the envious person's judgement becomes impaired, or his inclination is to engage in destructive or self-destructive behavior, then it could be considered a disorder: a psychological disfunction distressing or handicapping the envier, and possibly affecting the well-being of others around him. The truly malicious envier is unable to emotionally divest from the situation. Instead of focusing on himself, on moving toward a more desirable state, perhaps through self-improvement, he is only capable of directing his focus onto the envied person. His motivation is to bring the other person down or to destroy the perceived benefit that the other has acquired. The destructive path is set, and if intervention is not forthcoming, destructive consequences for him, the envied person, the thing desired, or any combination thereof may occur.

One possible course of action often witnessed or assessed in workplace settings but possible in a social context is "social undermining." That is, "behavior intended to hinder the ability of others to establish and maintain positive interpersonal relationships, work-related successes, and favorable reputations." [71] In this situation, the envier acts to interrupt or sabotage the envied person's relationship with, or reputation among, her contemporaries, her workmates, or her relationship with management. If she is the envied person's manager (again, usually within a first or second-tier level), then harming her superior status is the envier's deleterious goal.

If the malicious envier is prone to physical means as a way of resolving conflicts or just 'loses it' from the psychological stress he himself incurs from his chronic envy, then violent behavior may result. The murder of a desired love interest whose affections are given only to the envied person and not the envier is an extreme yet all too common example. Hence, malicious envy has different levels of intensity and, as one would expect, intense envy is likely to lead to more intense attacks, violent or otherwise, against the envied person or the desired thing. It is "the gap between the perceived limitations and inadequacy of the self and the imagined fullness and plentitude of the object,

[that] explains the intensity of the envy experience." [72] The less likely it is that the envier will ever be able to attain the desirable thing that the envied person has, or how unlikely he is to achieve a level of equality with the other, the wider the perceived gap will be. When frustration in closing the perceived gap is great, destructive behavior is more likely to follow.

It should be mentioned that aside from destructive behavior toward the other person or oneself, there is a more passive result that can occur either by itself or in combination with outward behavior. This is *Schadenfreude*. It is a German word that loosely translates to something like "sorrowful happiness," and is the feeling of joy that the envier experiences in witnessing another's misfortune. Like most aspects of malicious envy, schadenfreude is not something most people would be proud to admit they are experiencing. More likely, if they are prone to comment in the first instance, it would be expressed in the form of *"so n' so got what she deserved,"* even if what she "got" was something that no one deserves. "The man who is delighted by others' misfortunes," wrote Aristotle around 350 B.C., "is identical with the man who envies others' prosperity."

Envy, Wealth Redistribution, and "Fairness"

Wealth redistribution is the salient and persistent platform offered up by the modern American Progressive, including the Congressional Progressive Caucus and the Democratic party. Wealth redistribution is the concept of paying for government-funded social programs with taxes collected from the citizen's earned income, a corporation's revenues, or the gains a person realizes after risking her money by investing it in shares of businesses registered on the stock exchange (and/or other similar sources). By promoting and advocating for political platforms that support concepts such as Universal Basic Income, "free" government-sponsored childcare, "free" college education, and so on, the Progressive movement is by default advocating for higher taxation to pay for these programs since–for practical and theoretical purposes–"nothing is free."

If a police officer waives over a taxicab driver carrying a paying customer and extorts part of the fare for himself, perhaps by threatening to ticket the cabbie (as happens in many developing nations with ineffective law enforcement) most would simply *intuit* that isn't fair. It doesn't take much mental effort to figure that out. Yet, while the notion of fairness (which Progressives use interchangeably with notions of "equity" or "social justice") and deciding what is ultimately fair may *feel* intuitive, it can be much more complicated than that. Whereas most people can intuit what is generally fair or not – like the equal application of laws–often one's notion of fairness is subject to multiple, conflicting principles and experiences. For this reason, the question of "what is *fair*?" "What is *socially just*?" Or "what is *equitable*," when asked in the context of a given set of facts and circumstances will often yield multiple different answers (some radically different). "It's just not fair!" often appears at the conclusory stage of any Progressive argument for wealth redistribution and, predictably, higher taxation. Progressives seem to believe only they can intuit and serve as the ultimate authority on what is fair, just, or equitable on any social issues, including wealth redistribution. It's been a fallacy promulgated by academia since the early 1970s.

Philosopher John Rawls came up with his "theory of justice" in 1973.[73] In his explanation, he had a hypothetical that he considered demonstrated a universal truth: that humans could *intuit* what is fair and how a fair social system should look: not surprisingly, one in which everyone in the collective is essentially equal and where social justice reigns. However, and like many political and social systems, in theory, the gap between his premises and proven human behavior, i.e., the way humans "*ought* to act as compared to the way they *do* act" (to paraphrase Machiavelli) was too great. Rawls spent several subsequent decades pointing out the flaws in his own theory.

As to whether humans can simply intuit what is fair, consider a simple example of a custody and support case in a court of law. The mother tells the judge, "Judge, my ex cheated on me and therefore he should not have any visitation with our two toddlers. I think that is fair and equitable." Meanwhile, the husband says to the judge, "Judge, I should not have to pay so much in child support from my wage earnings. My wife should get a job at night after taking care of our kids all day. That would help lower my child support amount, and I think that's fair and equitable." Aside from the fact that no one is considering what's best for the children but only for themselves (i.e., that all children should have the benefit of having two caring parents and sufficient monetary support), neither side is being very fair or equitable. That a spouse cheats on his partner has no relevance to his right to help raise his children and anyone who has cared for small children knows that it *is* work and it comes with a high opportunity cost. Yet, the mother appears to be influenced by her bitterness, and the father by selfishness in thinking that caring for small children is not comparable to work. Neither party considered the other's circumstances or even their children's best interests. Such is common, not expected, and to a realist totally understandable as people are simply self-interested beings. They may sometimes be unclear as to what is really in their best interests, but self-interested all the same.

While lower and middle-class Progressives will rally around the notion that everyone wealthier than them needs to pay more of their "fair share," a sense of fairness has been found to be an insignificant motivator in those who support wealth redistribution. [74] Rather, those who actively or passively support the Movement's platforms advocating for increased wealth redistribution appear to be motivated by either of three emotions: *dispositional envy, self-interest,* or *dispositional compassion.* [75] As mentioned, the use of the predicate *dispositional* distinguishes the frequency and consistency of the occurrence of envy in the course of a person's life activities, i.e., the person who can be said to be always envious – Francis Bacon's "envious man" who walks the streets prying into others' affairs in order to compare them with his own. That person's envious disposition may or may not rise to a disorder or neurosis, as it were, but is distinguished from the episodic or occasional envier.

In a 2015 political psychology study conducted in Montreal, researchers conducted twelve tests with nearly 7,000 participants. Whereas they found notions of fairness to *not* be a significant player in one's motivations to support redistribution, self-interest *was* a prominent motivator. In other words, those who were likely to gain from wealth redistribution in whatever form were of course more likely to support it. The study asked those participants in the U.S. to select the political party with which they most identified, either Democrat, Republican, or Libertarian. The results showed that "self-described Democrats endorsed redistribution to a greater extent than Republicans and Libertarians did," and also reported "more expected personal gain from redistribution" than those who identified with the latter two politically right of center groups. [76]

The study also considered dispositional compassion, either by donating one's own money, food, or other resources to the poor directly through charitable contribution to either religious or nonreligious causes or by supporting government wealth redistribution programs for the poor's benefit. Interestingly, an increase in personal support for government redistribution "was associated with lower charitable contributions to religious or nonreligious causes." In other words, those more apt to support wealth redistribution were less likely to have donated their personal goods, money, or other resources to charitable causes.[77] The study concluded that aiding the needy through charity is predicted by compassion alone, i.e., without the emotional motivators of self-interest or envy. Support for wealth redistribution, however, could include all three.

And then there is envy. The results of the Montreal study do not flatter the envier, and envy was associated with both sides of the political spectrum (although the breakdown was not reported, including between self-identified Republicans and Libertarians as compared with simply "Democrat" respondents). In short, the participants were asked whether they would rather support

a) *a smaller tax rate on the rich but which would result in the poor receiving an increased amount of money than they presently receive from redistribution, or*

b) *a much higher tax rate on the rich that would result in cutting the present amount of money the poor receive in half (justified by an economic rationale that would result*

*in the rich ultimately generating less taxable income and
therefore less money would be available for redistribution).*

Nearly twenty percent of the American participants selected
the latter 'wealthy-harming' option even though it would result
in cutting the current monetary assistance to the poor in half. An
increase in a unit of envy, they concluded, was associated with a
much higher increase in preferring the second 'wealthy-harming'
scenario. Whereas Progressives support "economic justice"
platforms by loudly invoking notions of fairness in relation to
socio-economic status, race and gender identities, ethnicity,
immigration status, and other "intersections," their motivations
seem to lay in both self-interest *and* dispositional envy. Regarding
the latter emotion, the desire to harm the envied upper economic
class was so strong that it didn't matter if that harm resulted in
harm to others – i.e., to the detriment of those who were supposed
to benefit from wealth redistribution the most.

Case Study: Progressive Envy and the "Windfalls of Wealth:"

Francis Bacon was correct in his assessment of the envier
as a 'busy body.' For the envier by necessity needs to know who
around them has some better, more desirable object than they
do – be it prestige, wealth, or something else. The need to find
out who has what, even if it requires some digging, is a common
trait of the envy-prone person.

On May 28, 2021, opinion columnist for the Boston
Globe, Marcela Garcia, like Bacon's "envious man" had done
some digging around in personal affairs other than her own.
She found, "[i]n this Commonwealth of haves and have-nots,

throngs of millionaires inconspicuously live among us." Garcia had seemingly uncovered that "Massachusetts had about 18,000 residents whose annual income was more than $1 million..." [78] She had not only found these "inconspicuous" state residents out, but she also determined that they had not even earned this money or their wealth. Rather, her perception of these "haves" was that they had acquired their wealth and income,

"...through windfalls generated by innovations in biotech, startups scaling to maturity, venture capital partners deploying capital, and full-fledged technology companies churning out cash and stock options — all part of an ecosystem that derives from and feeds off of the state's research universities and other leading institutions. Wealth also abounds from our world-class financial services firms. Then there are the corollary services — real estate developers and law firm partners — and less flashy wealth in manufacturing firms and family-owned businesses you've never heard of that quietly earn millions." [79]

Garcia's overall argument in her opinion piece was, of course, that her rich neighbors should be made to pay more taxes to make things "fair." To shore up her opinion she offers the above passage, only not as a logical premise as to how paying more in taxes will benefit the state or its communities, but rather in order to justify emotionally that taking more money from other people's earnings – which is what taxation does – is ethical in this case because those people did not earn or deserve it in the first place. As we will presently see, deciding that the envied other gained his advantage or the envious thing–here a million-dollar income–unfairly is the malicious envier's first step toward destructive behavior.

Do we know whether Garcia's opinion piece was motivated by her envy of her "rich neighbors" in Massachusetts? A look at some of her word choices in the above paragraph alone might indicate so. She seems dismayed at "venture capital partners" for *"deploying* capital," tech companies for *"churning* out cash," and at "law firm partners," and "less flashy" manufactures, specifically small family-owned businesses. Garcia seems to be dazzled by all the flashy wealth and money going in every direction but toward her. "Deploying" connotes something in the nature of a military conflict, and her reference to "law firm partners" is a stereotype that, reminiscent of Bender's reference to male courtroom "bravado," might have come from streaming too many shows about prestigious and adventuring big city "power" lawyers. She likely has no clue as to what "venture capital" is and the irreplaceable service it provides for startup businesses that intend to produce something that they believe will be marketable – i.e., something needed and valued by consumers – but which they cannot fund through more conservative banking loans. Banks are hesitant to loan money to "ventures" that may result in losses rather than gains if the venture fails. Without "venture capital," those small businesses and their potentially revolutionary ideas and products might never exist. How tech companies *"churn* out cash" is unclear, but as *churning* is a legal term in the financial industry that describes the unethical and unlawful practice of creating commission income based on excessive trading in an investor's account, it sure sounds good.

Essentially, Garcia is arguing that her Massachusetts neighbors are not worthy of their accumulated wealth and or high income: that they just didn't *earn* it, and so for the collective good, they shouldn't be allowed to keep it. However, her concluding remarks offer the telltale sign that the envy emotion is quietly at work behind her motivation:

"Those who have been blessed with financial success at a level that most of us can only dream of ought to pay more for the common good so that many more people would have more opportunities."

If, as Garcia says, she "can only dream of" having the level of financial success as a millionaire or creating a million-dollar family-owned business, then by inference, these things are for her – or perceived by her to be – unattainable. There is the required or perceived gap between her and her supposedly wealthy neighbors. Seeing them with that level of income is simply unacceptable, emotionally consuming enough that she was compelled to expose this supposed unfairness in her column. Certainly, she is not immoral enough to rob these residents outright but advocating for higher taxes on income that is *already* taxed wealth is an easy moral justification if she can convince not only herself but her readers that these neighbors got to that level of income "through windfalls." Arguing that requiring these "rich" neighbors to redistribute more of their wealth "for the common good so that many more people would have more opportunities..." appears as a noble, "egalitarian" cause, but appears to be meant to disguise what seems clear as her own envy.[80] She portrays herself as one arguing for the less fortunate and, of course, for the good of the Collective, but as the PNAS study demonstrated, it is more likely that her motivation is not due to a sense of fairness but of envy. [81]

Envy and Moral Disengagement

In broad terms, there are two main camps when it comes to morals and ethics: the *deontological* and the *teleological*. In the first camp, it is one's actions in and of themselves that define what is right or wrong in any given situation. For example, a deontologist may say that one should never tell a lie, no matter what the circumstances or the result that is sure to follow. The teleological person may, on the other hand, argue that telling a lie is fine in some circumstances, as long as the result is something desirable for the common good. Doing something that most would consider being clearly immoral, like leaking a Supreme Court draft opinion, to the teleological person may not be immoral–so as long as in the end something may be achieved for the greater good.[82] Thus, "the ends justify the means" is a common phrase used to describe the teleological, and when viewed through an ethical lens, the actions of the American Progressive Left tend to comport with teleological ethics.

In the socio-political context of the Progressive Left, the means are not little white lies, but extreme moral justifications made by otherwise common people to, for example, justify their engaging in antisocial behavior. It is essential in convincing themselves that their destructive behavior, including property destruction and violence, is morally acceptable because of the potential social benefit that could be achieved. This viewpoint can help them believe they have the 'moral high ground' and emotional license to act. And engaging in destructive behavior because of envy often relies on such a justification.

Since Helmut Schoeck's early and comprehensive treatment of the envy emotion, psycho-sociological research regarding its various aspects and effects has advanced considerably.[83] In the course of their work, researchers have identified how it is that a person who normally adheres to sound moral principles – principles that self-sanction against harming others, and policing one's own behavior during emotionally charged situations with sound moral principles as a guide – can in the throes of envy wish for and cause harm to the envied person.

If the ends justify the means, then assaulting a political rally-goer by throwing urine, eggs, or frozen water bottles at her head is ethically justifiable. If violence prevents the victim and, more importantly, deters others who are terrorized by the assault on her from attending the same rally, then the Progressive is morally right. Brutally clubbing non-violent people who are opposed to one's "anti-fascist" worldview is ethical if one's own worldview is sure to provide the most good for the most people. Graduating from law school and then firebombing police cars to protest the law is a moral imperative if it promotes "equity." [84]

One's moral opinion of himself can be a strong deterrent to anti-social behavior. A strong moral base is often sufficient to keep a person from intentionally harming others. It's the Golden Rule you might say, and it is part of that "moral fabric" that cohesively holds a peaceful society together. This response is also known as self-sanctioning behavior. In many situations, it prevents one from engaging in destructive behavior without requiring the assistance of law enforcement. *"I couldn't live with myself,"* one might say as an expression of self-sanctioning, *"if I were to do such and such..."* How would I feel about myself if I were to vandalize someone's else's property because of my envy, one might ask. *I don't spread lies about others or try to sabotage their reputation,* another might say, *these things are below me. If I were to do these things, I would come to despise myself.*

However, when prompted by an envy emotion that they cannot control or counter through self-reliance, people who normally act quite morally can set out to cause harm or injury by abandoning any attempt at self-sanctioning. Between the formation of the malicious envy feelings and the carrying out of such destructive behavior, the envier goes through a psychological process of mentally distancing herself from the envied person. Incrementally, it appears, the malicious envier methodically convinces herself that the envied person is so undeserving of the envied thing, that harming him in some way that will ultimately deprive him of it, or his enjoyment in it, is morally acceptable. At the extreme, depriving the envied person of the desired thing is not just acceptable, it can become a moral imperative, righteous and in furtherance of, for example, "social justice."

The cognitive process used in this metamorphosis is called *moral disengagement*. Moral disengagement allows the envier to justify acting on his envious feelings while avoiding the self-sanctioning that would normally deter him from acting so.

Specific to envy, but with the same effect of devaluing the targeted person, is the belief that the thing envied, for example, a better income or employment position, a good reputation or prestigious social position, a superior skill set, even a quality neighborhood setting, etc. was bestowed upon or acquired by the envied person unfairly. That person did not earn these things, the maligned envier convinces himself, and therefore does not deserve to have them. This devaluation during the transition to total moral disengagement can occur over time "as [enviers] begin to ruminate obsessively on what they perceive to be the undeserved advantages of the envied others while ignoring the role that they themselves play in creating the disparity." [85]

That role, passive or active, can include bad choices, different priorities throughout the course of life, or the conscious or unconscious decision to not engage in self-reliant behavior. "Envious individuals may use euphemistic language to sanitize what normally would be considered antisocial behavior (e.g., 'making things right' or 'making things fair') and may also disengage mechanisms against antisocial behavior through advantageous comparison – for example, by rationalizing that their deviant behavior is minimal compared with what others have done to gain advantages." [86] Again, this rationalization is evident in Garcia's op-ed in the Boston Globe, *supra*, in which she literally argues that the flashy "rich people" in Massachusetts did not earn what they have and therefore she and others like her are justified in calling for them to pay more of their "fair share" for her readers' benefit.

In the extreme case, moral disengagement allows the envier to commit harmful acts "while avoiding the self-sanctions (e.g., self-condemnation, self-loathing) that ordinarily deter such behavior." [87] Some techniques or mechanisms used in the disengagement process should be quite familiar, like dehumanization. Dehumanization is a well-known precursor to, and arguably a factor in the fomenting of, violent conflict. The process includes referring to a potential or current adversary or enemy in ways that make them less human in the minds of both the combatant and the eyes of society. Referring to Jews as "rats" and "parasites" through not only speech but other visual and creative arts mediums served to allay the crimes against humanity by Hitler and the Nazi SS, as well as their approval in the minds of the German people and Fascists in other countries, including the local Nazi Ustashe's in Ukraine, Romania, Hungary, and Croatia. The systematically sadistic atrocities visited upon the Jews, Roma, and Slavs by the Nazis and their foreign equivalents were themselves so disgustingly inhuman, that today calling someone a "Nazi" is intended to impart an inhuman quality on the targeted recipient that results in some moral justification of hostile behavior against them, to the extent that such behavior may be contemplated by the name-caller or even a sympathetic observer.

Moral disengagement's role in the malicious envy process may help explain why Progressives tend to exhibit *schadenfreude* from the suffering of the political right, including those that it perceives have acquired advantages, tangible or otherwise, without deserving them. Why Progressives are more prone and easily moved to politically or socially motivated violence – not specifically during riots that arise from other causes, such as frustration at real or perceived injustice of, for example, police brutality and violence, but in physical assaulting and in some instances murdering (or in the case of Steve Scalise, attempting to murder) conservatives or supporters of conservative political candidates. There can be found a certain sadistic glee exhibited in social media conversations and even a subtle to not-so-subtle justification in mainstream media when violence occurs against the politically right of center victims. In all respects, the conversations are characterized by condoning the behavior as justified. The amount of violence against Trump supporters, the attempted shutdowns of roads and highways prior to rallies, property destruction, the pelting of Americans with eggs, water bottles filled with urine, and similar attacks – including vicious assault and murder during riots and unrest in traditionally Democrat cities is characteristically out of balance.

Case Study: Groveling Goblins and the "Poors"

New York Times contributor and self-proclaimed "lawyer by training, journalist by vocation," Sarah Jeong serves as a good example of malicious envy and moral disengagement in action. Jeong's social media outrage against "rich people" is an example of how the moral disengagement process works in the context of Progressivism:

"[d]umbass fucking white people marking up the internet with their opinions like dogs pissing on fire hydrants," she wrote. [88]

And then,

"[a]re white people genetically predisposed to burn faster in the sun, thus logically being only fit to live underground like groveling goblins." [sic.] [89]

Obviously meaning to dehumanize white people as genetically akin to "dogs" and little "goblins," she appears to be focusing on those that are self-reliant, risk-takers – who risk investing their earned wealth by financing others' business endeavors through the Stock Market. Like the Globe's op-ed author, Garcia, Jeong appears envious of those "rich" who she perceives have more money than her:

"...all the stuff you see about inflation in the news is driven by rich people flipping their shit because their parasitic assets aren't doing as well as they'd like and they're scared that unemployment benefits + stimmy checks + 15 minimum wage + labor shortage is why ~jmt~" [sic.] [90]

"...very spooky scary to think of the moment the poors realize inflation favors debtors and that that's what the hubbub is about, and not milk prices..." [sic.]

"...waaaaah the working class's income is keeping pace with or outstripping inflation but my capital gains aren't boo fucking hooooo..." [sic.] [91]

And like those whose egalitarian Thing was to "Occupy Wallstreet," for example, Jeong seems to misunderstand what a financial "asset" is or how basic economics, including "capital gains" and inflation, works. She appears to project a degree of *schadenfreude* in the financial losses of those "rich people flipping their shit." Is it that financial prosperity that she perceives as unattainable but envies? Is the fact that others' "parasitic assets aren't doing as well" emotionally gratifying? Either way, her demeaning language in context is a step in the *moral disengagement* process, convincing her social media audience that the *"[d]umbass fucking white people,"* those *"groveling goblins,"* who she believes collectively represent "the rich" are undeserving of what she likely considers as their envious advantage in life.

Ultimately, "through the process of moral justification, harmful behavior becomes acceptable because it is viewed as valued or righteous. In this way, envious individuals may begin to believe that social undermining behavior is not only condoned but appropriate." [92] Assaulting an otherwise innocent and defenseless person, most would agree, can never be morally justified. It is the quintessential example of antisocial behavior, and when it occurs the perpetrator is never revered as a hero by any public or community standard. However, if the perpetrator can devalue his target, i.e., morally disengage from the victim by reconstructing her in the public eye as someone who is not innocent, but deserves the assault that he has, or will, perpetrate upon her, then he and the community may consider that the perpetrator was justified, perhaps even *morally obligated*, to assault his victim. She was only getting, after all, what she deserves. This is precisely the route taken by the Nazis and countless other groups in pogroms and massacres throughout history.

In the public square, moral disengagement seems to be an anything-goes affair. After one's own party or movement has already determined and labeled the other party as "Nazis," "fascists," "racists," "homophobes," and so on, it's much easier to justify an attack on a perceived member of that party. Frozen water bottles flung at the other political rally attendees, the use of chemical sprays, knives, clubs, and then firearms are much more easily used on others when they are known to be emotionally less than human. How, after all, can a "homophobe" be considered human? Assaulting these 'submen'–say the club-wielding cavemen–is not only morally right but a moral obligation to protect the community or even the world from fascism. As in 2020 Seattle and other cities, moral disengagement is sufficient to allow in the name of righteousness the murder of the innocent in the streets as long as it furthers Progressive ideology.

And it is much easier to murder someone or harm her in other ways for her political views when you don't know her. Moral disengagement is that much easier when we don't have a close relationship with the victim. For example, many will attend a protest intent on physical violence – whether that intent is pre-meditated before the rally or after the rally is in progress and the situation turns conducive to violence. It is much easier for the normally self-sanctioning to commit violence when he does not know the victim. After the violent episode is over, the perpetrator may again be in the company of family and friends who do not share his political leanings. He may not like their differing point of view, political arguments may ensue, and he may even break off or limit relations in some instances, with parents or siblings. Yet, he is unlikely to attack them violently with a hammer, throw bricks at them, or try to get them fired from their job.

The Progressive's mantra of "white privilege" is another disengagement tool. *"[T]he Republican fascists (and their "centrist" allies embedded within the Democratic Party),"* wrote one Progressive pundit at Salon Magazine upset that President Biden had not yet forgiven student loan debt, are *"a group of sadists determined to cause maximum harm to the American people as a way of obtaining, keeping and expanding political power…[t]heir almost-explicit goal is to create a 21st-century Herrenvolk society in which Black and brown people, to quote the infamous words of Chief Justice Roger Taney, have no rights the white man is bound to respect."* [93] The Salon author attempts to shore up his argument with what seems a paranoid projection – calling the political right "fascists," and "a group of sadists," and (like the leader of the People's Temple discussed in Chapter Six) with a prediction of a coming society in which "Black and brown people" will be persecuted by having no rights.

This is not the first attempt to consider envy as a potential emotional driver of a person's political views. Sociologist Helmut Schoeck made this suggestion in the 1950s in his comprehensive study of envy. [94] Envy can and often does lead to deleterious and destructive behavior, Schoeck realized, but while envy is an individual psychological issue, "it is also a sociological problem of the first order." [95] Schoeck observed that the influence of envy "as the implicit or explicit fulcrum of social policy [is] much more destructive than those who have fabricated their social and economic philosophy out of envy would care to admit." [96]

Schoeck was specifically referencing contemporary movements in both Europe and the United States that espoused Marxist Socialism and Communism. The inference is that Socialist Communists are primarily motivated by envy informing and promoting their "social and economic philosophies" according to its tenets. Take, for example, a *command economy* – one in which the individual's efforts are severely limited and stymied through government regulations that restrict one's natural ability to produce or talent to create, and in which the government substitutes itself as the rational being in the supply and demand equation. According to Schoeck's viewpoint, envy in this case would be the "implicit fulcrum" upon which a command economy is set because of the Socialist's awareness that he is so inferior inability to the free market entrepreneur.

For the Progressive and his cultural Marxist notion of class conflict that is so essential to bringing about the Collectivist Utopian society, envy serves a critical role toward that end. Whether the classes in conflict are identified by wealth, power, race, or gender, "the determinants of dispositional envy," will have "consequences on the intrapersonal, interpersonal, and societal level" that can all be exploited by the Progressive Marxist, because "dispositional malicious envy may contribute to societal conflict. In sum, dispositional envy appears to be an important personality variable contributing to the regulation of status hierarchies." [97]

The Progressive constantly attacks those he deems to be "rich" and those on the political Right by arguing that their success, wealth, position, etc. – either real or perceived – are the result of undeserved advantage. "You didn't build that," a Progressive and self-proclaimed "reformed Marxist" President Obama informed a group of small business owners, "somebody else built that." Your success in life, however minimal, is because you are white, your "white privilege" led to your success, not your hard work and self-reliance. It's because you're a man, or a Capitalist clearly against "the poors" that you have succeeded.

Aggravating the matter is the growing number of young people who have college degrees, but for whom the number of jobs requiring such degrees is declining. That is, "over the past twenty years we have created twice as many bachelor's degrees as jobs to employ them." [98] Many of those earning bachelor's degrees don't find employment or positions that require a degree, any degree. They graduate from college but compete with high school-educated kids for work. Not only are their preconceptions of economic success after college dashed, but they also increasingly become more frustrated with "the system." Higher rates of "incarceration, as well as drug, alcohol, and other health issues" ensue. [99] For these, Capitalism is the culprit. The gap becomes significant and unable to alleviate it through self-reliance, critical social theories become more appealing. It is, again using simplistic rationalization, "the rich" who must pay their fair share so that these degree holders can have a fairer chance at opportunities. Socialism is the solution, and if it takes one party fascism to enforce it, then so be it.

This growing number of underemployed and overeducated are not inconsequential to the Progressive movement. During the two decades following World War I, "[t]he vast majority of the population, was seized with the feeling of individual insignificance and powerlessness...." [100] "Nazism never had any genuine political or economic principles," wrote Fromm, "the very principle of Nazism is its radical opportunism. What mattered was that hundreds of thousands of petty-bourgeois, who in the normal course of development had little chance to gain money or power, as members of the Nazi bureaucracy now got a large slice of wealth and prestige they forced the upper classes to share with them. Others who were not members of the Nazi machine were given the jobs taken away from Jews and political enemies, and for the rest, although they did not get more bread, they got 'circuses.'" [101]

Collectively, they got total destruction.

Envy helps explain the motivations of those who fall for the American Progressive movement's mantras demanding "social justice," that "the rich" pay their fair share, that people should not be allowed to own their own homes, [102] their adamancy that no one should own a gun for self-defense or, for that matter, defense against a tyrannical government. By denying people the right to keep more of what their labor has earned them, by seeking to divest normal people in what is likely their most precious and common investment, i.e., one day owning their own home, and wanting to keep them from owning a weapon to ensure that no one, private or public, can take wrongfully take away their freedom or their life without an equal defense, the American Progressive's deep psychological need to control the individual in favor of the Collective can be fed, although hardly satisfied.

Envy, though present, is not explicitly identified in Progressive social theories, including communism and neo-Marxist "critical" theories such as critical gender theory, critical race theory, and critical fat theory. They will shout "Tax the Rich!" but they will never shout "Tax the Rich because I am *envious* of all the wealth they have," even though this is implicit in the ease and comfort they have in taking more and more of the income or, as of late, the previously taxed 'wealth' that an individual has accumulated in the course of his or her life. Hence, Progressives often disguise their envious desires as moral or egalitarian concerns. The Progressive will explicitly and unashamedly shout "The rich didn't earn that money or wealth themselves, and therefore they don't deserve to keep it!"

One reason that envy is never explicitly recognized by Socialists is because it is so despised by society. It is an extremely difficult emotion to admit to having. That is, it is relatively easier for a person to earnestly admit to another that he feels guilty for having done something harmful to someone else, or to honestly admit that a colleague at work angers him so much that he would like to meet him in the proverbial dark alley. It's even easier for a sincere person, for example, a lover, to admit to his significant other that she is jealous of another woman who was flirting with her lover – the possible loss of the lover's undivided attention is unfathomable. However, it's not so easy for a person to admit with the same sincerity that she is envious of another woman who has as a lover someone that she herself desires and would try to take for herself without hesitation, or that a colleague at work has been granted some benefit of which she is truly envious to the point of ill will.

The Left certainly does not have a monopoly on envy. Envious persons come in all shapes and sizes, as well as political beliefs. However, when such persons who are prone to uncontrollable, disproportional envy form into social groups, leftist ideologies are fertilized. Success in establishing socialism and communism relies heavily on the manipulation of the latent envy emotion of persons who are prone to not only evoking it but becoming obsessed with it. However, as a general proposition those on the further reaches of the Right side of the political spectrum, through the value that they place upon self-reliance, are less likely to rely on envious feelings than those on the Progressive left side of the spectrum. Those on the political Right, including those who value Individualism and self-reliance in countering the less desirable effects of emotion, simply do not exhibit that same frail tendency toward malicious envy and moral disengagement. Arguably, those on the Right appear to not envy anything that the Progressive has: not their success, not their moral value set, and certainly not their inclination toward the inconsistent, non-universal application of logic and reasoning in socio-political matters.

The Progressive's envy-induced frustration causes a desire for vague, authoritarian measures to force all those who benefit from individual freedom to surrender it. The solutions can only be destructive, dismantling anything considered "systemically" racist. Perhaps eliminating the electoral college – to further the move to one-party rule like all Fascist and Communist systems. This time with the densely populated Progressive urban areas dictating political and social decision-making for the rest of the population. Better yet, eliminating the current Constitution altogether, teaching young children that it's just outdated, so therefore we need a new one. [103] But then the same frustration arises because the Progressive theorist cannot even begin to think deep enough to deliver even a conceptual vision of an alternate document. With all the arguments to the contrary, she becomes hypersensitive to other's free political speech and demands their silence by claiming that the other's speech is 'offensive' and even 'dangerous.' This gives her some time to think, in her safe space, but the barren soil of ideas bears no fruit. Slowly she sinks into more contradiction and frustration. She searches for 'the Thing' in which she can feel safe: perhaps a revolution, the anti-racism movement, 'economic justice,' or Climate Change. She can become a warrior for a higher cause and thereby forget her intellectual deficiency. For the hardcore Progressive any means to divide by class – racial, economic, gender – is meant to cloud cooperative human interaction. This she uses to her tactical advantage. But in the name of equity and egalitarianism, her envious emotions remain obvious.

Countering Envy with Self-Reliance

As debilitating and destructive as malicious envy can be, it can also play an extremely positive role. If the potential for envy is in all of us as part of our biochemical make up – part of our evolutionary heritage–then why are all of us not looking at our neighbors, friends, and colleagues who have something we desire but can't have? Why are we not secretly (or notoriously) despising them or suffering depression because of the perceived gap? While most people do at some point experience envious feelings, perhaps even unconsciously, most of the time it is *benign*. As opposed to malicious envy, when envy is present benignly it "may have positive consequences if, for example, it motivates a person to increase performance or attempt self-improvement." [104] This is the "healthy competition" effect, i.e., seeing what another person has acquired or achieved and instead of seething or setting out to destroy him or what he has, focusing inward on oneself with the goal of attaining that desirable thing or state by improving oneself.

Various studies demonstrate this. For example, a 2015 study that found *dispositional benign envy* [105] "predicted faster race performance of marathon runners mediated via higher goal setting," while in contrast, "dispositional malicious envy predicted race goal disengagement." [106] In other words, whether *dispositional* (part of one's personality or disposition) or *episodic* (only occasionally envious) those who experienced benign envy set higher goals for themselves to better compete with, and challenge, those similar to other runners whom they envied. By doing so, they improved their own run times regardless of whether they beat the envied, superior runner's time. In the context of social or personal status gaps (when the envier desires the other's superior economic or perhaps reputational status) "people who are inclined to experience *benign envy* make more positive impressions on others, improve their performance, and, ultimately, reach better well-being." [107] Quite the opposite of malicious enviers who, as the study of marathon runners demonstrated, "disengaged" in what was essentially self-defeating behavior.

What factors influence who experiences malicious envy and who experiences benign? There are likely many, including emotional intelligence and social development beginning in early childhood. After all, that *neurocomputational* calculus of human psychology has many formulas. That notwithstanding, the process of motivating oneself to improve in a meaningful way meant to close the gap between the envied other is called *self-reliance*.[108] When a self-reliant person experiences envy, she is less likely to resent or even focus on the object of her envy – the envied person–or harbor ill feelings or ill will toward them. [109] Self-reliance is recognized as the most common and effective means of envy mitigation, the envier relying upon "emotional control, perseverance, and tenacity."[110] Whatever the desired object or condition is, the self-reliant person determines to harbor no ill-will toward the superior or similar other, i.e., the envied person, and focuses instead on improving her own performance and relying on her own motivations. Those who experience dispositional benign envy, who can mitigate their envious emotions through self-reliance, are less likely to experience, e.g., *schadenfreude*, when the envied person suffers a misfortune of some kind, whether related to the envied thing or not. [111]

"Rugged self-reliance" has for centuries been used to describe freedom loving Americans and their independence of thought and action. It is something that most people – throughout history and including outside observers like Tocqueville–admire. For to be self-reliant is the first step toward being free – physically and spiritually. Learning to be self-reliant begins at an early age and most Americans by the time they reach the age of majority – sometimes much earlier – are well on the way to some degree of self-reliance. "God helps them who help themselves" is oft-invoked rule of thumb, i.e., who rely on themselves first and foremost. Some learn that "if you want something done right, then you have to do it yourself," or if things don't go right the first time, well, then learn from your mistakes and do it right the second time. If you fall, don't wait for someone else to pull you back up. Try first to pull *yourself* up, as we say, "by the bootstraps." Since others in our communities may have to depend on *us*, then the best thing for the community that we can do is to learn to be as self-reliant as possible and not to be a drag on the community, but a contributor with little to no dependence on government.

It is interesting to note, however, that by 2020, many Progressive schoolteachers who had bought into Critical Race Theory's shaky tenets were teaching that "the Bootstrap Theory" (as the Progressives had now pejoratively termed self-reliance) was a subversive and "racist" concept.[112] Progressive theorists promoted the notion that the virtue of self-reliance is not universal or to be celebrated by individuals of all colors or ethnicities. Rather, it is another systemic tool of oppression meant to keep white people 'in power.' Teaching kids to pull themselves up by their bootstraps, they believe, is racist because black and brown children do not have a "'can-do' attitude" and are not "goal-oriented."[113] Whatever the motivation for including this notion in Progressive theories, its obvious effect will be to discourage self-reliance in young people and reliance instead on the government. And the more one relies on the government, the less self-reliant she is and the less individual freedom she will have. Perhaps this is the intent.

Chapter Five

Fear

"He is afraid of engaging himself in a project as he is afraid of being disengaged and thereby of being in a state of danger before the future, in the midst of its possibilities."

> – Simon de Beauvoir, The Ethics of Ambiguity

"The transition from the democratic to the totalitarian system is easy when indefinite fear paves the way. The way back is likely to be difficult..."

> – Kurt Riezler, The Sociology of Fear, 1944

In the years following World War II, sociologists and psychologists sought to determine how the rise to a historically unparalleled "European Fascism" had occurred. How the citizens of those nations that espoused it had allowed its rise. Many observers found peace of mind by concluding that Fascism's dynamic rise was due strictly "to the madness of a few individuals." Other observers felt secure in believing that the people of these Fascist nations simply had not had time to make the successful transition from a Feudalist social mentality to a democratic one. Democratic principles would take hold in time, they believed, and such would prevent the rise of fascism (at least in Europe) again. Still, others believed that the peoples of these nations were dragged into fascism only by brute force and fear: against their will and powerless to will it otherwise.

However, psychoanalyst and philosopher Eric Fromm concluded early on that these theories were simply fallacies and wishful thinking. The last belief, i.e., that the citizens of the Axis nations had accepted Fascism unwillingly, Fromm considered the most dangerous to perpetuate. "Millions in Germany," he argued, "were as eager to surrender their freedom as their fathers were to fight for it: that instead of wanting freedom, they sought for ways to escape from it..." In other words, a large part of German society eagerly welcomed Hitler as "the Leader" and his notion that all must sacrifice everything for the collective good of the German people. In response, many Germans seemed to willingly forfeit their individual freedom to be part of an authoritarian, controlling regime.

What Fromm and subsequently other sociologists and psychologists came to recognize is that many people when faced with the fear of an uncertain future – a characteristic of modern societies that stress freedom and liberty–are quite susceptible to a deep-seated psychological yearning for security. Fear of isolation, of being left to one's own devices to survive in the modern world, is a constant worry.

For the typical American Progressive, the future threat may not be immediate, but he still perceives it to be existential: the physical destruction of the world by Climate Change caused by unseen factors of personal failure in a social system that values

Individualism, self-reliance, and freedom. While Capitalism and the economic and spiritual freedom that accompanies it has demonstrably lifted hundreds of millions of people out of poverty, there are still those – even many who are otherwise well off within a society that promotes it–who fear that "grant of liberal freedom" which causes, as Hitler noted, so many of them to "easily feel deserted." The modern Progressive fears the modern world she lives in.

Freedom does come with what can become an overpowering feeling of aloneness: alone to plan one's successful future, to chart one's own course, but also to suffer the losses if one is not successful or unable to become self-sufficient. Psychologists and sociologists generally recognize that in modern society, and particularly in Capitalist countries, people often feel lost in what seems like a wilderness, one in which life is often characterized by insecurity and loneliness. A person may be able to realize her wildest dreams of success, but first she needs to survive. This feeling of aloneness can become overbearing, and arguably dispositional fear with its ambiguous anxiety caused by the unknown takes hold. If it is strong enough, it becomes a neurosis constantly seeking relief. It is "the inability of the isolated individual to stand alone and his need for a symbiotic relationship that overcomes this aloneness." The object of this "symbiotic relationship," as will be discussed in a later chapter, is often the Collective and a strong authoritarian government that the individual perceives will care for him or her by providing direction and managing as much of their affairs as possible, so they need not worry about "starving to death on the street" in the future.

Indefinite Fear

Medieval Europeans may have been born into a feudal caste system – the largest tier not so free as serfs and commoners – but for all the socio-cultural inhibitors placed upon them starting at birth, there was a certain security in the knowledge of their life's clear social boundaries, and the limits of any individual expectations they may have had.

Americans in our current state of unprecedented liberal freedom lack this comfort: life's course is not laid out before us at birth like it was for those in feudal Europe. There is no single road that we can be expected to travel. Modern woman's destiny may not be marriage and children, or even as a homemaker. Instead, she has the opportunity, even the expectation, to choose her lot in life. She's now expected to work–even if she does marry–and contribute to the family income. She may go to college after high school and pursue a particular career path or join the professions like being doctor or lawyer or enlist or seek a commission in the military. It's the same for young men, of course, and the choices are many and varied. Ultimately it is he who is expected to go out and make his own way in life and, still the hope of most parents, to make them grandparents. Success (however one defines it) is never guaranteed in a free society. Becoming self-reliant – traditionally the defining characteristic of Americanism and American culture (i.e., "rugged self-reliance") is still an expectation for many Americans.

For others, however, self-reliance is not something desirable but more of a penance. Progressives appear to exhibit through their various social and political platforms a fear for the security of their future in a free, Individualistic society. Often disguised as a concern for the future of others, particularly the "working class" or certain racial or gender groups, the modern Progressive Active Supporter tends to lack that self-reliance that is critical to making one's own way without any, or a minimum, of government help and assistance. They believe that most people cannot make it without government: with the help of the Collective that government represents. Unexpected illnesses require federally funded and universal healthcare for all. A lack of funds in a downturned economy or just the stress of paying a mortgage or rent each month requires Universal Basic Income. Universal daycare for the babies, and "free" community college for all – just in case twelve years of public secondary education wasn't sufficient to prepare one to be self-reliant.

For many Progressives, things like Universal Health Care and Universal Basic Income will help allay their fear of being left alone. These become, for them, "basic human rights." Some, like Speaker Nancy Pelosi, believe they are enumerated in the Constitution. Pelosi was never clear exactly where it is enumerated in that document, but Progressive pundits have assisted by simply narrowing it down to the Ninth Amendment: "As a non-lawyer," John Graham admitted in the National Review, "my understanding is very simple: The Ninth Amendment states that 'the enumeration in the Constitution, of certain rights, shall not be construed to deny or disparage others retained by the people.'"[114] Using very circular reasoning to support UHC, Graham invokes the common fallacy in claiming health care is already a "certain right...retained by the people," and thus the Ninth Amendment prevents the government from denying or disparaging it.

"[W]hat we call 'health care' today did not exist in the 18th century, so there was no incentive for the Founders to enumerate a 'right to health care,'" he continued. What we call Universal Basic Income didn't exist in the 18th Century either, so according to Graham's logic the Ninth Amendment makes that a right also. Because there is an apparent "incentive" today, perhaps because Progressives agree that UHC is equitable or indicative of "economic justice," then it should naturally be a right is the Progressive argument. Graham then compares this new right to medical service as equally fundamental as the right to practice one's religion or to speak freely.

As mentioned, of course, no service or commodity – things that someone else through their labor must ultimately provide or produce–is free. For Graham to have a right to free health services, somebody else will need to work to provide it to him or pay for his medical service by having their income taxed at a higher rate (or both). For Graham to practice the "religion of his choice," on the other hand, does not cost anyone else anything. Similarly, for Graham to exercise his right to free speech, which he apparently does, costs everyone else nothing. No tax money is necessary for him to speak about the Constitution and rights, or for that matter to exercise his right to bear arms. No one need be taxed for Graham to pay for the gun of his choice.

The distinction is huge and one that Graham and other Progressives constantly miss. If one person is required to work or pay for you to exercise your "right," be it healthcare or welfare, then it is simply not a right; not a civil right nor a human right. If it requires taking someone else's money, i.e., to which the laborer or risk-taker arguably has an equally justifiable right, then it simply does not fit the definition of a right. Like it or not, one has no right to demand that another person work to provide him something of value: health services, more family time, or art supplies.

Universal Basic Income or Universal Health Care, the Progressive movement supports both wealth redistribution platforms. For the individual Progressive, including here the passive supporter, both platforms promise to offer a degree of security: the Progressive need not fear being left to pay for these services himself. Only with government help will he "not starve on the street" or die if he becomes ill. These things, as well as other redistribution platforms, help allay his fear of living in what must seem like the proverbial wilderness, always fearful that he will be left to his own devices for survival. As such, fear is the chief motivator behind his self-interest in supporting redistribution. Although the Montreal study, supra, did not attempt to identify the core motivators of those who supported wealth redistribution as a matter of self-interest, it is not unreasonable to believe that fear was a motivator. Getting 'free stuff' is always pleasing (if its good stuff), but why, as the study found, do those on the political Left support redistribution more as compared to those on the Right, i.e., than those who value Individualism, self-reliance, and other similar Libertarian values more? To the extent that the individual on the political Right does tend to value these concepts more, both philosophically and in practice, more likely than not it indicates a lower fear factor in the psyche of those politically right of center.

The Congressional Progressive Caucus has also been able to effectively capitalize on another aspect of indefinite fear through the promotion of Climate Change theory. This uncertain future calamity, although promoted as all but inescapable if drastic measures, like banning all U.S. fossil fuels permanently and ending the consumption of most red meat, are not begun as soon as within "twelve years." For the Progressive, Climate Change serves as a future possibility akin to Christianity's concept of Hell that can only be avoided by self-sacrifice and atonement in the present. Fear of Climate Change has been extremely effective in selling the ideals of the Progressive Green New Deal: a body of regulation that is essentially a Collectivist supplement to a command economy and a more powerful regulatory government. It is the Progressives' call to action, comparing themselves to allied forces during World War II.[115]

Intersectionalism: Identity Lost and Found

Without the self-reliance, independence, and self-confidence to welcome individual freedom, those who fear living with freedom in an Individualist society become "obsessed by doubt." They not only yearn to rely on and find security within the Collective but as a direct result begin to lose track of their own individual identity. This results in an emotional panic: fear that he will remain "insignificant." In the face of this identity crisis, From notes, "[h]e is compelled to conform, to seek his identity by continuous approval and recognition by others. Since he does not know who he is, at least the others will know, and he will know too, if he only takes their word for it."[116] His doubt in his identity compels him to make, as de Beauvoir put it, "[n]ever positive choices, only flights," and in the reflection of the Collective "[h]e will proclaim certain opinions; he will take shelter behind a label; and to hide his indifference he will readily abandon himself to verbal outbursts or even physical violence. One day, a monarchist, the next day, an anarchist, he is more readily antisemitic, anti-clerical, or anti-republican."[117]

The Progressive is lost in a world of freedom that makes her feel insignificant and a world of emotional and theoretical contradictions that provide her no solid footing. Without a steady moral or ethical foundation, she finds herself compelled to overly rely on others, not least of all "the Collective," to find her identity. She is taught by Progressive academia and activists that she can only find and "affirm" her identity by associating herself with social groups with whom she shares various, usually immutable, physical characteristics. But this is a fraud. Instead of finding her identity in terms of individual character traits, like honesty, integrity, diligence, kindness, compassion, or bravery, the Progressive is taught that her reality is with the identity group or groups to which she belongs. Whatever the group appears to be or stands for, well that pretty much sums her up too.

Enter the Progressive notion of "intersectionality" that pervades Progressive philosophical thought, Critical Theories, and Social Justice notions. "Intersectionality," writes one Progressive proponent, "is a way of understanding and analyzing the complexity in the world, in people, and in human experiences. The events and conditions of social and political life and the self can seldom be understood as shaped by one factor... Intersectionality as an analytic tool gives people better access to the complexity of the world and of themselves."[118]

In intersectionality, the individual identifies with various groups with which he or she shares immutable characteristics, but to determine or ascertain a specific level of discrimination that the person, it is assumed by him or her sharing these immutable characteristics, has suffered. Our experiences of the social world are shaped by our ethnicity, race, social class, gender identity, sexual orientation, and numerous other facets of social stratification. Some social locations afford privilege (e.g., being white) while others are oppressive (e.g., being poor).

"When it comes to social inequality," writes another Progressive in Marxist class struggle terms, "people's lives and the organization of power in a given society are better understood as being shaped not by a single axis of social division, be it race or gender or class, but by many axes that work together and influence each other."[119] Social inequality, the theory goes, is the only factor without which a person can never have "true knowledge" of himself. Individual identity simply cannot exist without the Collective's experience of oppression and domination "affirming" it. And it is the Collective that will ultimately decide whether one's intersectionality identifies him as an oppressor or (more esteem worthy) one eternally oppressed.

Not surprisingly, Progressives embrace this notion of identity and inject it into their politics. It developed concomitantly with modern "critical theories" that began appearing and getting academic attention in the 1980s to remedy salient social issues. The concept was allegedly coined by Kimberle Crenshaw in 1989 in a paper she wrote for the Stanford Law Review arguing that, whereas, generally, all women have historically been the victims of male domination, which is true and a major premise of Feminism, that black women have been historically marginalized within feminist theory itself because of their race. When people think of feminism, for example, they think only of white women. Furthermore, black females have been marginalized in the "antiracist" movement as well because of their sex. Thus, concluded Krenshaw, black females are more oppressed than both white women and black males because of the black female's "intersections" of race and sex. Crenshaw's argument might not be unsound, but like all theories, intersectionalism's usefulness as a tool to help resolve social problems was much more tenuous and vaguer. However, many Progressives in academia jumped on the bandwagon, not wanting to be left out of mapping new "intersectionalist" based analyses in the search for Social Justice, particularly one that promised to define anyone who was looking for an identity, and even those who weren't, in terms of oppressor and oppressed.

In a sort of academic entropy, it was not long for more identities to appear and intersect. Besides gender and race, economic class, religion, nationality, age, transgenderism, queer affiliation, physical weight categories, social hierarchy levels, immigration status, and nativity, as well as the degrees of one's skin complexion (light brown to black) began to bestow a particular hierarchical degree of oppression that defined one's identity and experience. Identifying with as many historically marginalized or oppressed groups as possible is a reaffirmation of oneself and a means to achieve certain self-esteem as reflected back from the view of the Collective. As a result, one's personal accomplishments and individual character begin to take a backseat to identity. For the Progressive, intersectionalism is another essential concept that can be used to implicitly affirm the non-sequitur that, not only was America founded on racism and oppression, but that the same oppression still exists "systemically" as evidenced by so many intersectionally oppressed people.

Case Study: Encouraging Intersectionalism in Children

There has been much debate as to whether and/or how much "Social Justice" education is being imparted now in elementary and secondary public schools throughout the Nation, and in particular with respect to one of its major subdivisions, Critical Race Theory (that teaches that all American institutions, including the Constitution, are "systemically racist" against several identity groups). For Progressives, identity and intersectionality are critical in understanding the oppression of all "identity groups." Schools or Progressive teachers who peddle these theories try to convince children that their own identities are dependent not on character or personality traits, but on their immutable physical or religious characteristics: those that connect them to one or several identity groups. There are many for-profit and non-profit organizations that provide classroom materials and tools to help teachers with this effort.

One such tool is an Identity Worksheet that a Progressive teacher in Maryland apparently "adapted" for her students to determine their own identity. On the top, the instructions explain to the student that "Identity encompasses the memories, experiences, relationships, and values that create one's sense of self." The purpose of the worksheet is to assist students in "finding" their identity in three easy steps:

First, the student is provided a list of "Traits/Characteristics" that included "gender, ethnicity, race, religion, socioeconomic status, language, and sexual orientation." Of course, none of these are personal traits or characteristics, i.e., a feature or quality belonging to a particular person. They are in the main social group identity characteristics and it's obvious that the intent is really for the student to determine their social group identities or intersectionality.

Second, the student is told to finish the sentences, "I am…, I can…, I have…, I remember…, I like…, I will…, I believe…" As an example, the instructions state "if the statement begins with 'I am…' you can complete the sentence by saying 'a student,' 'happy,' 'a runner.'"

Third, the student is instructed to "copy and paste" their statements in the second part that "fit neatly into the categories" on the first chart. So, if say a student wrote "I am bisexual," then he would put that into the chart next to the row for "sexual orientation." Thus, we presume, the student believes he has found a clue to his identity – his sexual orientation and that he is bisexual.

However, there seems to be an apparent incongruity that likely exposes the teacher's editing of the worksheet to fit the Progressive identity narrative. For example, responses like "I am…a runner," "I will…run a marathon," or "I am…happy," do not immediately fit into any of the social group categories. A foreseeable problem can arise, one which is indicative of the emotional and psychological toying in which Progressive K-12 educators are engaging, consciously or not. That is, what of the child who writes responses like, "I am…a really good student; I can…play video games all night long. I have…a dog who loves me. I remember…camping with scouts. I like…reading travel magazines. I will…work this summer, and I believe…that people should be honest." None of her responses "squarely fit" into any of the identity categories. Has she no identity? Would we expect the teacher to say soothingly, "Oh it's OK, lots of people don't have an identity?" Or would the teacher give her a little urging, say maybe go back and change a few responses to insert her skin color or how much her father or mother earns each month so she can identify with a racial or socioeconomic class?

Obviously, the Progressive teacher's intent in "adapting" this identity exercise to her intersectional matrix was to inculcate the notion that one's identity is based on one's association with groups that share race, sex orientation, socio-economic status, gender, etc. Success in the teacher's mind, it can only be imagined, would be for a child to finish the exercise and say with surprise, "I'm a middle-class, black, cisgender, English speaking male. Wow, I knew it all along!!"

In his treatise on the nature of mass movements, Eric Hoffer posited that joining such a movement required a person to be first "stripped of his individual identity and distinctness." Hoffer explained that this occurs with "the complete assimilation of the individual into a collective body." In fact, this is a central goal of communist indoctrination techniques and is often facilitated by group "self-reflection" sessions in which prospective recruits to the movement – typically with heavy peer pressure – stand up and renounce their inherent selfishness that compelled them, before the movement taught them otherwise, to think only of their own self-interests and not to selflessly sacrifice for the Collective. He must be taught to believe that he is nothing unique and that his only value is being part of the Collective. The paradox is that "being essentially a reflex of other people's expectation of him he has in a measure lost his identity." To find his identity in the reflection of race, gender, immigration status, weight, monetary wealth, or lack of it, the Progressive has forfeited his true individual identity.

The fear of surviving a "liberal grant of freedom" was a deep psychological affliction in many living in pre-War Germany that Hitler recognized and was able to capitalize on to attract the population to his National Socialist Party. Fascism with its emphasis on the safety, security, and anonymity of Collectivism could and did, offer to allay this fear. Joining the Nazi party or actively supporting it provided meaning, significance, and a sense of security for the insecure individual. It promised a degree of pride, power, and, not least of all, some amount of control for those occupying even the lowest positions in the movement and with the power of the monolithic party behind him. Ultimately, in the case of Nazi Germany, it resulted in not only the power to commit genocide but a move toward national suicide.

That similar or even greater grant of liberal freedom that most Americans have and thrive on today is still intimidating for those whose "identity" is tenuous, fragile, or based on reflections. For them, they inwardly, perhaps implicitly, perceive no advantages to freedom. In fact, "they may be antagonistic toward freedoms and people who exercise freedom."[120]

Freedom can, admittedly, be an intimidating concept: one is on one's own and must make the best decisions for him or herself "come what may." One decides what is best and if it's a poor decision or a poorly executed decision, then one suffers the consequences. This is not to say that there should be no safety net, as most neo-liberals would suggest, but even with all that the government, between local, state, and federal provides, there are those who are still unsure and fearful of a future with freedom. For the Progressive, the fear of not having an authoritarian government to care for them is the cause of much anxiety. This is not to say that government has no role in preparing and saving for those events that cause temporary needs, which neoliberals would agree is a legitimate purpose of limited government. For the Progressive, however, the need to feel secure and cared for increases progressively with each new related legislation, almost like mission creep or a drug dependency. One's entire life and needs are insured by the Collective from birth to death: universal daycare to a Universal Basic Income to Universal Health Care.

"Spirit is the journey," sang South African songwriters, Johnny Clegg and Juluka, "and body is the bus; I am the driver from dusk to dusk." For Progressives who fear a "liberal grant of freedom," it is simply much more comforting if a higher authority does the driving. Certainty is what the Progressive craves, and most often that comes in the form of a controlling, paternalistic, Authoritarian government that "knows what's best for the Progressive and all its citizens."[121]

CHAPTER SIX

Guilt

"Hatred is useful in fomenting a war which does not seem to be occurring of itself."

– Francis Yockey, Imperium, 1948

W e have all felt guilty at one time or another, for having done something that we should not have, or intentionally failed to do something that we should have, and which caused someone else some degree of unnecessary harm. With true guilt, one feels discomfort and even emotional pain for having *caused* some other person (or sometimes an animal) some type of harm. It is often accompanied by a desire to repair the damage one caused or to make amends in other ways if the damage is irreversible. Apologies are forthcoming if their delivery is still possible, and perhaps we try to do some unsolicited kindness to make amends – "to right the wrong"–even though doing so does not completely dispel the anxiousness we feel since one can never completely nullify what one has caused either physically or, perhaps, by hurting another's "feelings."

And it is causation that is a necessary precursor to evoking the guilt emotion. That is, the guilt emotion arises naturally only when *we* do something harmful to someone else. We don't feel guilty for someone else's harmful acts, but only for our own. This principle applies – or should apply–to nearly all relationships in which we may find ourselves. For example, if a family member, perhaps a brother or sister, injures someone: we don't feel guilty for their harmful act or for the harm done. We may feel empathy for the injured person, or even for our sibling if he or she may be feeling the pain of guilt. Similarly with our friends who intentionally or unintentionally cause harm to another. If we didn't have control or influence over their actions, and we ourselves did not cause the harm that they inflicted, then we should not suffer emotional guilt. The same is true with a parent – if they are otherwise functioning adults whose act was not the result of our negligence in caring for them. We may suffer embarrassment, sympathy, or other emotions, but not true guilt.[122]

In law, of course, guilt is used in the objective sense and not so much in the emotional sense. A finding of guilt by a judge or jury – hopefully after hearing and considering the facts – results in an objective conclusion that the defendant did in fact commit some wrong, either one *malum in se* (an act that is inherently evil or wrong, like rape) or *malum prohibitum* (one that is not evil but still prohibited, like fishing without a license). If determined to be guilty, some reasonable punitive measure should follow. In theory, punitive measures are not meant to simply *punish* the guilty person. Rather, they are meant to accomplish one or a combination of three things: protect the community by getting the offender off the street if he or she poses a danger, to rehabilitee them, and to deter others by serving as a warning to those who might be inclined to engage in the same unlawful behavior.

However, in the subjective sense, a person found guilty of committing a crime may experience remorse for having done so (assuming she is in fact guilty). Often at the end of a hearing – during the sentencing phase – a convicted person will exercise their right to express that remorse, e.g., for "having made a bad decision," or "being sorry that he has caused injury to the victim," etc. To the extent that one actually means it and is not just trying to get a more lenient sentence, they accept responsibility for their act and the chance to "pay their debt to society." In such an emotionally honest person, there is a true sense of guilt for having committed, and commensurate with the gravity of, the act. They are repentant and willing to pay their fine or do their time.

Enter the efficacy of the guilt emotion in the fostering of a mass social movement. "The technique of a proselytizing mass movement," noted Eric Hoffer, "aims to evoke in the faithful the mood and frame of mind of a repentant criminal."[123] Hoffer considered that a mass movement's "unity and vigor" requires a sacrifice in the mind of the movement's support for a "poignant sense of sin."[124] If the potential supporter is not a criminal, which of course most modern Progressives are not, no matter: the technique is "to infect people with a malady and then offer the movement as a cure."[125]

Hence, the guilt emotion plays a special role in the furtherance of the modern American Progressive Movement. Progressive activists in academia, the press, and social media daily strive to instill such a "poignant sense of sin" by convincing the crowd, especially the young, that they are guilty of their "privilege," their "whiteness," for slavery, for "colonialism," or simply their "intolerance" in believing, for example, that mammals can only be male or female. Activists continually

stress the fallacy that the country was created in order to perpetuate slavery, and its institutions, from the Common Law to
the Nuclear Family, are "systemically racist," and to support any
of it makes one a racist – a condition for which she must atone.
[126] If successful, she must credit not her own determination and
effort, but that of others. She "didn't build that. Somebody else
did." She should feel guilty for having gained so much on the
backs of others.

Guilt has been documented as extremely effective in Socialist
and Communist recruiting efforts, as well as maintaining the
system once adopted by the target society. During the Cold
War, Chinese, Northern Korean, and North Vietnamese "political officers" instilled false guilt with several objectives. First
was to recruit and quickly indoctrinate supporters and fighters
amongst those who were not apt to join the revolutionary effort
of their own volition. They employed small "self-criticism" sessions where potential recruits were singled out one by one to
stand in front of the group and discuss how they had committed
the "crime" of, for example, only have thought of themselves in
life, for having lived only "selfishly" and for not having acted
for the good of the Collective. With the spotlight on them, the
shelter of anonymity was lifted, and sincere or not, others were
affected by the speaker's confession, sense of guilt, and desire
for atonement. Similarly, during the Korean War, Chinese cap-
tors instilled such a strong feeling of guilt in American prisoners of war that, immediately after repatriation U.S. Army
personnel processing the released POWs quickly noticed the
sullen, depressive moods in many, and an inability to make eye
contact or conversation with fellow prisoners.

Today, American Progressive theorists offer a smorgasbord
of guilt from which its supporters can choose and offers itself

as the remedy: an almost religious venue through which its supporters can atone for their supposed sins by becoming an "anti-racist," and "anti-fascist" or simply one promoting "social justice." In all cases, however, the only way for ultimate atonement will be to surrender their Individualism to the good of the Collective. "An effective mass movement," Hoffer saw, "cultivates the idea of sin. It depicts the autonomous self not only as barren and helpless but also as vile. To confess and repent is to slough off one's individual deisticness and separateness, and salvation is found by losing oneself in the holy oneness of the congregation." [127]

The Merit of Guilty Suffering

The problem is, of course, that no one living on this earth today was responsible for the institution of slavery, say between Biblical times and 1865 in America. The modern individual Progressive was never responsible for harming anyone through slavery. Although the early Progressive Movement adopted and approved of eugenics, including the efficacy of forced sterilization and abortion to slow the population growth of undesirable classes and races, specifically black Americans, the modern Progressive never engaged in institutionalized slavery or racism (with the exception of their current viewpoint that racists can be identified by the color of their skin). The modern Progressive's race-based guilty feeling is simply a fraudulent one. However, it appears to be one that she needs to feel.

Like fear and envy, the guilt emotion (whether artificial or natural) can prompt the "masochistic defense." In the 1920s Freud claimed that repressed (i.e., unconscious) feelings of guilt can lead to a palpable desire for suffering, either through emotional or physical pain. That people would willingly want to cause themselves to suffer by inducing pain in some form may seem to many as bizarre. How could inflicting pain on oneself make one feel better? Yet, Freud was able to identify the phenomenon, calling it "moral masochism."[128] Fromm, although he was critical of what he considered Freud's overreliance on the satisfaction of sexual urges as the basis for all human motivations, integrated moral masochism (and its constant companion, sadism) into his analysis of the rise of fascism. More recently, the desire to cause self-harm in response to feelings of guilt has been successfully demonstrated. [129]

Like other human emotions, what guilt feels like or when it should arise is not something that can be taught. Just as one can't be taught how to feel love, fear, loss, compassion, or hatred, neither can guilt be taught. However, otherwise innocent people – especially the young and adolescents – can be fooled into believing that they are guilty of some act when in fact they are not. If successful, the feeling can be just as powerful – and just as destructive–as the guilt derived from one's own wrongful act. For those inclined toward masochism, guilt can be just as emotionally satisfying.

Case Study: The matter of JEM

JEM was by all objective accounts a young American Progressive who, on her small business website page made it known to all that she was someone who "included" and did not discriminate against people of any other race, ethnicity, gender, sex, or "identity." She herself, however, was guilty of being white, and because she was an American, she declared, she struggled each day – "like all Americans"–with her own racism. Every day, she believed, she "reaped the benefits" of the color of her skin and "white privilege." JEM had a high school degree, and she made a meager living as an event photographer. That she had no education above public high school, and she did not lead a trendsetting lifestyle on her small income, did not seem to warrant her conclusion that, but for her "white privilege" she wouldn't be in the same economic position – i.e., economically in the same class she was now. For JEM, believing she was a *de facto* racist because of the color of her skin, her penance, her Thing, was to be an ardent "anti-racist." This was the only way to atone for her alleged sins and privilege.

She formed a Facebook page for local residents who could promote anti-racism and 'equity' in her neighborhood. She identified as a member of Black Lives Matter and wholeheartedly supported that cause. She made social media posts, for example, that she felt sorry for her black friends, and she dedicated her time to organizing and participating in anti-racism rallies. Although she had no children, she was a proponent of teaching the concepts of Critical Race Theory–that America is at heart a racist nation–in the local public schools. Anti-racism seemed to define her existence.

With the power of "anti-racism" behind her, her mission became clear: daily she perused social media, looking for anyone making comments that were antithetical to "anti-racism," to Critical Race Theory, or contrary to any platform promoted by Black Lives Matter, including "defunding the police." In one of her first attempts to control others' online speech, JEM read a post by a young man in the local community that condemned the "defund the police movement." The young man suggested that any woman who supported "defund the police" and found herself in danger of being raped would have no one to blame but herself if there were no police to respond to her 911 call. JEM found out where the young man worked – in the restaurant industry–and began emailing his employer, alluding that he was a sexual predator who was making "uncomfortable remarks online about raping women." She further explained that she herself was a patron of this particular restaurant and was in the habit of referring her photography clients there. The employee's remarks, however, had made her so uncomfortable that she felt compelled to notify the owner since she was sure that they didn't support that kind of thing. In other words, "fire this guy." He was in fact laid off while an investigation into his "online behavior" ensued.

Her next target was a local mother who had spoken out about activism in the public schools where her child was a student. The public-school superintendent happened to be black, and when the mother's social media posts, posts criticizing the superintendent for promoting Black Lives Matter and encouraging school children to organize and participate in protests, JEM was compelled to take righteous action. She began texting and emailing the woman's employer and encouraged sympathetic others to do the same, and they did: alleging that the woman was a racist, that she was 'inciting violence,' and how could the employer tolerate such behavior. Again, the message was clear: fire this person.

Both of JEM's targets sued her for defamation and related causes of action in state court actions. During sworn testimony, JEM explained that Americans, including her, struggle each day with their racism. That the only way not to be a racist, was for a person to commit herself to "anti-racism." However, when asked what the definition of "racism" was, JEM had no answer. Two of her most outspoken online supporters who had encouraged and, as to one of them, also contacted the mother's employer, when asked under oath had no definition of racism either. "I don't need a definition," one of them stated, "I just know it when I see it." JEM and her compatriots had all convinced themselves – or more likely they got played into believing – that they and every other white American were inherently, systemically guilty of racism even though none of them could define it. As Hoffer had concluded in his analysis of effective mass movements, this was Progressivism's "idea of sin," and its remedy was atonement by being an active "anti-racist."

JEM did not *appear* to be a racist – she obviously did not believe that her own race was superior to another (the definition of racism), she did not appear to consider other races as inferior, and she had African American friends in high school and maintained those friendships into adulthood, and most telling, she was just normal as far as her chosen livelihood and lifestyle. She had not derived significant wealth, status, education, or political position – nothing that anyone could conclude was due to her "white privilege." Yet she felt "guilt" for having earned or attained what she did have – somehow believing that she had had a definite advantage over those of other races.

Guilt is a very uncomfortable feeling and is often intense enough to satisfy the masochistic personality's desire to feel pain. It also serves the Progressive's goal to recruit for the cause by attempting to create a false, or *faux*, guilt complex in others. Hence, it is both a means of achieving the emotional pain that produces the pleasure response for the masochist and a tool to indoctrinate those who are either willing to accept it voluntarily or who are very young and easily influenced, like many K-12 and, apparently, college-aged students.

And an uncontrollable sense of guilt, real or not, can lead to the masochistic defense and self-defeating behavior. "[M]asochism is the ego's way of submitting to the object in hopes of being forgiven for the crimes and offenses that have evoked the object's punishment. In this way, masochism is hiding the aggression that caused the attack against the superego's boundaries as well as engaging in an attempt to propitiate the angry superego." [130] With guilt, "masochism operates as a means of disguising the hostility against the object by debasing the self."

CHAPTER SEVEN

Moral Masochism

"Liberals actually hate wealth because they hate all success. They hate success especially, of course, when it's achieved by other people, but sometimes they hate the success they achieve themselves."

– P.J. O'Rourke

The Depressive Masochist

A s with many emotions, envy, fear, and guilt can be the sources of great anxiety, sadness, depression, and even self-hate. As we have seen, most people learn to deal with them, mitigating their potentially disabling effects. We put up with these uncomfortable feelings while trying to understand our own fears and insecurities. We try and make amends if we have needlessly or carelessly caused someone injury for which we feel guilt. At other times, we turn our uncomfortable emotions toward some positive outcome, like the self-reliant envier, to improve ourselves by focusing inward, closing the perceived gap by self-improvement rather than trying to injure and bring down the one we envy. It is only when we cannot successfully mitigate their potentially destructive effects, when they persist in becoming all-consuming and negatively influence how we act and interfere with normal living, that they may cause a mental disorder.

Exactly when one begins to suffer a mental disorder depends completely on the situation and peculiar circumstances facing a particular person. There is no precise boundary of observable behavior – indicators–that can accurately determine when a person can truly be diagnosed with a mental disorder. Neither is there a sufficiently accurate definition of *mental disorder* itself: "*distress, dyscontrol, disadvantage, disability, inflexibility, irrationality, syndromal pattern, etiology, and statistical deviation…[e]ach is a useful indicator for a mental disorder, but none is equivalent to the concept, and different situations call for different definitions.*" [131]

Masochism (and Sadism) are commonly thought of in the context of sexual erotica or, in psychology, paraphilia. The Diagnostic and Statistical Manual of Mental Disorders describes sexual masochism as an urge or behavior that "involves the act (real, not simulated) of being humiliated, beaten, bound, or otherwise made to suffer," which causes or satisfies sexual arousal. [132] A form of sexual masochism is "hypoxyphilia," which involves sexual arousal by oxygen deprivation and has caused death in many instances when the means of deprivation are misapplied or malfunction in the course of sex. [133] Whereas some may engage in masochistic behavior over the course of many years, if not their lifetime, without an increase in the injuriousness of their acts, others may increase the severity of the suffering, leading to physical injury or death. [134]

The phenomenon of masochism, however, is not restricted to sexual behavior or psychology. Psychologists have recognized *personality types* who find certain satisfaction and enjoyment in their own emotional suffering–an implicit need to punish oneself. They take pleasure in, and seek out their own defeat, subjugation, and ultimately their own spiritual or physical domination by someone perceived to be a more powerful other. The masochist has learned to hate himself and often turns to self-destructive, self-defeating behavior to undermine his pleasurable experiences. He is not incapable of feeling pleasure, but often his self-inflicted pain and suffering are meant to, and are necessary to, bring about such pleasure. Ultimately, physical or emotional pain creates the desired feelings of pleasure.

Moral (or spiritual) masochism is a much more profound phenomenon and distinguishable from sexual paraphilia. In moral masochism, the individual experiences an overwhelming emotional urge to *spiritually* merge with what he or she sees as a greater, more powerful force. It is often characterized as a symbiotic relationship, one with a psychological dynamic of losing oneself and one's individuality in the identity of the more powerful other... This merger of one's identity with the dominant object is typically characterized by "submissiveness, self-denial, and self-surrender" in the masochistic personality. [135]

As described by famed German psychologist Karen Horney, *"[Masochism] is a form of relating and its essence is the weakening or extinction of the individual self and merging with a person or power believed to be greater than oneself...a way of coping with life through dependency and self-minimizing. Though it is most obvious in the sexual area, it encompasses the total range of human relations."* [136]

According to Horney and others, masochism's ultimate end is the psychological or spiritual demise of the individual with his attempt to "merge" with or into the idealized, stronger power. That is, his own extinction, or what De Beauvoir referred to as "suicide."

Masochism eventually came to be recognized as a potential psychological disorder, to wit: Depressive Masochistic Personality Disorder (sometimes referred to as "Self-Defeating Personality Disorder" or the Masochistic Defense).[137] When true masochistic urges are sufficiently strong enough to interfere in the conduct of ordinary life activities or with one's relationships with others, it may be considered a mental disorder. By the end of the Twentieth Century, psychologists had identified connections between *chronically* experienced emotions, specifically including malicious envy, fear, and guilt, that could lead directly to the disorder. If the disorder was already present from these or other causes, uncomfortable emotions like guilt or envy could feed the masochist's need for emotional suffering since, as mentioned, certain emotions like envy are so uncomfortable that they have been "linked to the activation of neural circuitry that is responsible for physical pain." [138]

During the early part of the Twentieth Century–while modern psychology and psychoanalysis were themselves in their nascent stages–masochism was simply categorized under the umbrella of depression. For early psychoanalysts, it was just another symptom of a *character type* who suffered from "mood disorders" or who experienced a "constant emotional emphasis in the somber emotions involved in all the experiences of life." [139] Psychoanalysts soon began distinguishing, however, between those depressed character types who simply emphasized these "somber emotions" and an emerging, distinctive character type: one who is "predominately 'ill-humored.'"

This distinctly different character was not just melancholic with the inability to enjoy life but was "cold and selfish, grumbling and hateful, irritable and critical, even mean and ill-intentioned." These characteristics were not necessarily associated with known depressive disorders, but this personality type seemed particularly nasty in their relations with certain others:

"Their pessimism in the face of all things and also in regard of their own fate has something fanatical about it. They almost rejoice at new failures, and neither do they desire anything good for others."[140]

Not unlike those prone to dispositional malicious envy, many who fit this "grumbling" character type constantly compare themselves to others who seemed to be living life contentedly. They are critical of and often irritated "with those who live happily, and knowing the simplicity characteristic of such people leads them to consider suffering something noble and to regard themselves rather in an aristocratic manner...see[ing] suffering as a merit..."[141]

This "meritorious sufferer" is indicative of the "moral masochist" that Freud had first described in the 1920s. Because masochism requires an awareness of and a symbiotic merging with a stronger, more powerful other, the masochist is a self-depreciator, a self-defeater. This symbiotic relationship is caused by "an intense craving to absorb into oneself the values perceived in others," and "corresponds with the self-shrinking aspect of envy..."[142] Not unlike the malicious envier, often after a period of brooding disengagement from the object of his envy, moral masochists tend "to emphasize their concern for moral justice, thus attempting to justify it. Accordingly, they tend to describe their attitude as resentment rather than envy. It is clear, however, that this is a kind of rationalization of their negative attitude to being inferior." [143] Hence, he is constantly on the lookout for something "noble" for which he could martyr himself for the "merit" that would be associated with his suffering. This supposed sacrifice on behalf of others, would allow him to feel in a higher moral position, virtuous and "aristocratic."

For the moral masochist, the desired symbiotic relationship with a powerful other need not have as its object another person or authoritative individual. The object can be, and in the context of political psychology often is, some cause or social crusade that she perceives as noble, one for which she can dedicate herself through sacrifice. A social or political movement is often referred to as a cause, but Simone de Beauvoir in her book The Ethics of Ambiguity referred to a powerful other simply as "the Thing." "He suppresses himself to the advantage of the Thing," she wrote, "which, sanctified by respect, appears in the form of a Cause, science, philosophy, revolution, etc."[144] Eric Hoffer recognized the same motivation in a certain personality type likely to join a mass movement, one who sees self-interest as something "tainted and evil," and seeks self-worth through self-renunciation:

"Their innermost craving is for a new life – a rebirth – or, failing this, a chance to acquire new elements of pride, confidence, hope, a sense of purpose and worth by an identification with a holy cause. An active mass movement offers them opportunities for both. If they join the movement as full converts, they are reborn to a new life in its close-knit collective body, or if attracted as sympathizers they find elements of pride, confidence and purpose by identifying themselves with the efforts, achievements and prospects of the movement."[145]

It is the "respectable" Thing, the movement, from which the masochistic personality derives his new identity and self-worth. But there is also something more – the power of the Thing–for the masochist's desire is not only to lose one's identity through subservience but *to share in the strength and power of* the perceived dominant other (hence, De Beauvoir's observation that Nazism was both a lust for power and suicide at the same time). She may ultimately lose her own identity, but she expects to share in the other's power to control, and it is power and control with which masochists are in awe.

Like those Germans who felt an overwhelming desire to submit to the Nazi ideology, the moral masochist looks toward "dissolving oneself in an overwhelmingly strong power and participating in its strength and glory." [146] He need only submit and surrender himself to it and he will have the authority and the respect of the Thing behind him. It is the Thing that is the authority, the sole arbiter of all that is good. Once merged into it, he will have the authority of the powerful Thing for himself. He too, like the power of the Thing, will be able to exercise control over others.

And for the modern Progressive, the powerful thing comes in many forms, including "Anti-Fascism," Climate Change, "Anti-Racism," or "Social Justice," and she can be its warrior.

Sadism

Sadism is all about physical or psychological control, and many individuals diagnosed with chronic sexual masochism also engage in sexual sadism. That is, they derive "sexual excitement from the psychological or physical suffering of the victim." [147] In most instances sexual sadistic behavior is practiced with a consenting partner, often one inclined to sexual masochism. However, because sexual sadism (like masochism) is usually chronic, for those who engage in it with *non*-consenting {Note: pls italicize 'non'} victims, "the practice is likely to be repeated until the person with Sexual Sadism is apprehended."[148] In severe cases, "individuals with Sexual Sadism may seriously injure or kill their victims." [149]

In the socio-political context, the moral sadist craves control over others. The sadism of the German Socialist Fascists who were "drunk with power" over their own population and those of the areas they conquered, the dehumanizing treatment of different ethnicities and classes of people leading up to the maniacal murder of more than six million innocents needs little discussion here. Equally so with the efforts at population control and control over the individuals living in Communist Bloc and communist countries throughout the world. The ease with which crimes of extreme violence can be meted out in furtherance of communist movements and causes is indicative of the mass movement's masochistic desire for submission and rebirth as a powerful, all-controlling force.

"[T]he sado-masochistic person," wrote Fromm, "is always characterized by his attitude toward authority. He admires authority and tends to submit to it but at the same time he wants to be an authority himself and have others submit to him...." [150] He will then be ready to exercise his always present sadistic urge to control others. [151]

Case Study: High School Teacher Gabriel Gipe

A clear example of the moral masochist and sadist urges can be observed in the actions of a former California high school teacher, Gabriel Gipe. Gipe, whose social media page included a photo of himself with a Soviet hammer and sickle tattooed on his torso, was filmed by Project Veritas in 2021 proudly admitting that he was actively indoctrinating the students in his charge to become Marxists. [152] "I have one hundred and eighty days," gushed Gipe, "to turn them into revolutionaries." When the Veritas agent asked him how he does this, Gipe responded, "scare the fuck out of them."

This is a classic pattern of behavior demonstrating the sadist's uncontrollable desire to control. He will try to play upon anyone that he is able to control through fear and due to their weaker character or, in this case, position: the minor children who are required to be in his classroom. In his classroom, Gipe purportedly hung a picture of Mao Ze Dong and an ANTIFA ("Anti-Fascist") flag. Gipe, according to the Veritas video, boasted that he once "shamed" a student for taking offense at the ANTIFA flag. "I have an Antifa flag on my wall," Gipe claimed, "and a student complained about that and he said it made him feel uncomfortable… 'Well,' Gipe told the child, "This is meant to make fascists feel uncomfortable, so if you feel uncomfortable, I don't really know what to tell you. Maybe you shouldn't be aligning with the values that [the Antifa flag] is antithetical to.'" [153] Ironically but not surprisingly, it was Gipe who was acting like a Fascist. Hereby employing a false notion of guilt to convince an adolescent that he is an oppressor by "aligning with the values…antithetical to anti-fascism" in his effort to turn the child into a "revolutionary."

While Gipe used fear and guilt in his sadistic urge to control and ultimately indoctrinate school children, his complementary masochistic urge is evident as well. That is, the Thing to which he has made himself subservient–and judging from the hammer and sickle tattooed on his chest and the poster of Mao on his classroom wall – is Communism. These outward displays in which there appears to be a sense of pride, are meant to portray him as being a member of that higher, more powerful Thing. His mission was not so much to educate, but to indoctrinate the school children into becoming servants of the Thing too, here by having them engage in Communist and ANTIFA themed events, writing about their experiences for "extra credit," and "turning them into revolutionaries."

Case Study: Bake My Cake

In 2012, two otherwise unknown gay men walked into the Masterpiece Cakeshop in Lakewood, a suburb of Denver, Colorado. They asked the owner, Jack Phillips, to design and create a wedding cake for them in celebration of their upcoming same-sex marriage. Phillips refused, claiming that he did not believe in or support gay marriage since it was contrary to his own religious beliefs. As mature adults, the two men might have responded with something like "Oh, no problem. Well, do you know of any bakers in the area that might be able to do it?" Or perhaps a short and concise "F*** you!" would have been considered not unreasonable under the circumstances. But the soon to be married couple seemed not to have been self-reliant enough to react in a benign fashion. They needed something to affirm their otherwise obscure existence.

So, they complained to the Colorado Civil Rights Commission demanding that Phillips be fined until he designed their cake as ordered. *You WILL create our* cake, they were essentially saying, *or we're going to sue the hell out of you and ruin you and your family's livelihood.* For these two men, this cake was simply about forcing another human being to do something that they knew he did not want to do. Characteristically sadistic, they felt an overwhelming need to control the baker and to force him, to coerce him, to act according to their will. This was even sweeter since doing so would require Phillips to abandon something he held dear: his faith in God. The sadistic urge in them needed satisfaction.

And satisfaction they initially found, winning an administrative hearing in the Colorado Civil Rights Commission after Phillips refused their demands. One of the commissioners who ruled in the couple's favor against Phillips described religious freedom as something abusive that Phillips had used against them:

> *"Freedom of religion and religion,"* she claimed, *"has been used to justify all kinds of discrimination throughout history, whether it be slavery, whether it be the holocaust, whether it be—I mean, we—we can list hundreds of situations where freedom of religion has been used to justify discrimination. And to me it is one of the most despicable pieces of rhetoric that people can use to—to use their religion to hurt others."*

Directly citing this commissioner's emotionally irrational argument, the Supreme Court Justices found quite the opposite. They held that "the Commission's treatment of Phillips' case violated the State's duty under the First Amendment not to base laws or regulations on hostility to a religion or religious viewpoint." [154] After a long fight for what he knew was right, the couple's case was overturned by the Supreme Court as violative of the Constitution and the obligations that states have to uphold the Bill of Rights in respect to their citizens.

Phillips then became a target of another sadomasochistic Progressive: in the middle of the first nationally infamous controversy, a lawyer who also happened to be "gender transitioning," asked if Phillips could make him or her a cake–with blue icing on the outside and pink on the inside in order to celebrate his or her transition from a man to a woman. As he or she must have expected and desired, Phillips declined. The sadomasochistic urge took over, and to satisfy it she too felt the desire to make Phillips do something that he did not want to do. She filed suit in the local court, the baker was fined again by the same Commission, and it started over again.

Case Study: Lisa Layton and the People's Temple

Horney considered masochism as a potential force in neurotic character development. In that development, "masochism has its own special purposes and value system: suffering may serve the defensive purposes of avoiding recriminations, competitions, and responsibility...and a way of expressing accusations and vindictiveness in a disguised form." [155] Whereas envy and fear of personal responsibility can bring about the same neurotic character, guilt is a significant player in the development of moral masochism. Although guilt is a naturally occurring human emotion, in the context of the psycho-sociology of the American Progressive it is quite an artificial one. An uncomfortable and even painful emotion, guilt is one that the masochist can self-exploit. That is, guilt can satisfy the need for pain, here emotional pain, that the masochistic character needs in order to feel pleasure. Guilt provides punishment for the masochistic character for her real or imagined sins and crimes. [156]

The story of Mrs. Lisa Layton is instructive as to the guilt emotion, but also the interplay between sadistic control and the willing subordination of the masochist. Layton was a Jew born in Germany. In 1938, she was just a young girl in her teens living with her parents. They had seen the growing public hatred of the Jews fueled by the Nazi Party and had just experienced Kristallnacht – a premeditated and coordinated night of violence and destruction against the German Jews carried out by Nazi stormtroopers, Hitler Youth, and a sympathetic and actively hostile public. Although unlikely that her parents foresaw the scale of the horror of the Holocaust that was to come, they obviously knew things were going to get worse for Germany's Jews before they got better. They had enough money and foresight to get Lisa passage across the Atlantic while the borders were still open. Lisa never saw her parents again: they did not survive the Holocaust.

She arrived in America and with the help of family friends enrolled in college. While the war in Europe raged and the mass atrocities played out in death camps like Auschwitz and Buchenwald, Lisa met her future husband. Laurence Layton was a medical student, and the couple was later married. They had two children: Larry and Deborah.

After graduating from high school, Lisa's son, Larry Layton, attended the University of California at Davis. While there, Larry met Carolyn Moore, also a student, and in 1966 the two married. Larry had secured a military draft deferment as a conscientious objector, and in lieu of military duty, he was allowed to serve as a medical technician at the Mendocino State Hospital in northern California. Not far away, in Redwood Valley, Carolyn found a church with a sizeable congregation and a very charismatic Reverend. The church was called the People's Temple, and its leader was the Reverend James Warren Jones.

Jones habitually preached to his congregation about the inherent injustices of American society: the evilness of "the rich" and America's systemically racist society and institutions. The American government, the Reverend declared, was secretly building concentration camps in which it intended to intern Black Americans.[157] He was vehemently against the Vietnam War and paranoid that the U.S. government was spying on him and the People's Temple. [158] He was also an ardent Communist and believed that he himself was the incarnation of Lenin. [159]

All of this apparently appealed to Mrs. Layton's son and her daughter-in-law, Carolyn. They both joined the Temple and became dedicated followers of Jones. They eventually introduced Jones to Mrs. Layton and her sixteen-year-old daughter, Larry's younger sister, Deborah.

Mrs. Layton listened to the Reverend's sermons and his criticisms of the rich who he blamed for all the injustice and unfairness in American society. She began questioning her own status, her *privilege* for having married a doctor and in leading a life of relative comfort. She felt guilty that she had so much in life when there were others less fortunate. She became engrossed in her guilty feelings and "deeply disturbed by the family's growing affluence." [160] According to her husband, Dr. Layton, Lisa was "constantly bothered by feelings of guilt 'about having so much.'" [161] It appeared to him that Lisa was "a woman looking for a worthwhile cause within which she could submerge herself." [162]

Jones was also talented in deception, convincing his congregation not only to believe his paranoid projections about the U.S. government but also that he had special powers that he could heal cancer. Jones also held a powerful and controlling grip on his followers. Many of them felt that Jones would not let them leave the church once members, and through his charisma, many were convinced not to leave. When city and state elected officials questioned him regarding stories from some congregation members that they were not allowed to leave his church, he basically shrugged it off as people saying some things because they didn't like him. No more questions asked.

But Jones was also a sadist who had demonstrated at a young age a pronounced pleasure in controlling others and causing them pain. [163] During the subsequent investigation of the murder-suicide of some 900 members of his church in "Jonestown," Guyana, it came to light that Jones regularly engaged in sexual sadism with his followers, including with Larry's wife Carolyn who he was able to convince to divorce Larry while keeping them both dedicated followers.[164] Jones humiliated Larry by forcing him to engage in a degrading homosexual act in front of Carolyn.

Meanwhile, Jones had contacted Lisa Layton's other child, Deborah, while she was still in high school. He told her that after having met her, he could see that she had latent but powerful leadership potential. He wanted her to join his church when she was finished with high school. And as soon as she was, Deborah did: she became Jones' bookkeeper and eventually the church's administrator. After several years, she was Jones' second in command and came to know all the secrets of the People's Temple, financial and sadistic.

With his new commune, *Jonestown*, ready for occupancy in Guyana, Jones convinced some 900 of his followers that to escape persecution from the American government, they had to leave the United States. Lisa Layton cashed out her and Dr. Layton's life savings without his knowledge, some $250,000, and willingly gave it to Jones. She and nearly a thousand others then travelled to Jonestown and their socialist Utopia.

Several years later, Deborah realized that she needed to escape Jones and his commune. Fortunately for her, as Jones' bookkeeper and manager, Deborah had often had to fly back and forth from Guyana. On her last trip from Guyana, she met with representatives from the U.S. Congress, in particular California Congressman Leo Ryan whose constituents made up a large majority of Jones' congregation. Deborah testified in front of Congress and Ryan dispatched himself and his aide to Guyana to personally investigate. Ryan never came back. He and his aide were shot, Ryan some forty times, on the tarmac after having been given a tour of Jonestown that had failed in its attempt to portray the congregation as willing and free residents.

When Jones heard the news that the Congressman had been murdered (his aide survived), he knew his time was up and that the U.S. and Guyana authorities would be on their way. In the ultimate demonstration of sadomasochism, some 900 men, women, and their children willingly drank or were forced by others to drink cyanide-laced powdered juice aid, later referred to as "Kool-Aid."

Letters from Jones' followers during the existence of the Temple indicate that "[t]hey sought through this process to merge with their idealized omnipotent leader magically in the hopes of overcoming their lack of a positive self-image and corresponding healthy self-esteem. Unfortunately, the price they paid was that of a total masochistic surrender to the authority and will of Jones."[165]

In moral masochism, it is dispositional guilt, envy, and fear–all extremely uncomfortable emotions–that the masochist seeks to exploit to satisfy his need for emotional pain and suffering and through them, establish his self-worth. The emotional pain suffered by the masochist in this realm satisfies his psychological needs, not to feel suffering itself, but to feel the pleasure – often in a notion of self-worth – that the suffering brings. Suffering, in effect, can help the otherwise self-defeated personality demonstrate to others that she is worthy of notice, of virtue, of love, and other things she considers desirable, and which are, or which she perceives to be, out of reach. "By exaggerating and inviting suffering, it justifies demands for affection, control, and reparations. In the distorted value system of the masochist, suffering is raised to a virtue..."[166] For JEM, it was for allegedly unfairly reaping the benefits of her "white privilege" and her constant, self-debasing struggles with her own alleged "racism" that she had been taught to believe was inherent in all white Americans including herself. Her penance was to be a committed "anti-racist." She would ruin anyone opposed to her achieving that, i.e., "to use every force available in order to maintain linkage and fusion with the perceived source of all that is good." [167] Anything or anyone who stood in the way with that linkage or fusion, like the school mother, was a menace.

Chapter Eight

Collective Sadomasochism

"There is one simple rule that you should bear in mind: the psychopathology of the masses is rooted in the psychology of the individual. Psychic phenomena of this class can be investigated in each individual. Only if one succeeds in establishing that certain phenomena or symptoms are common to a number of different individuals can one begin to examine the analogous mass phenomena."

– Carl Jung, 1946

History and analysis have clearly shown that groups and associations "are capable of regressing to a group psychology..." [168] "Group think" is probably the most well-known concept that describes the behavior – often undesirable behavior – of the individual's inclination toward conformity and anonymity in the course of group decision making. Similarly, individuals can express feelings and emotions toward entire *groups* of people. Hatred of a particular group is a commonly expressed feeling, but so too can be jealousy, fear, or contempt. "[O]ne might envy all the wealthy people in one's community, for instance...the larger the group being envied, the more likely it is that the difference between the envier and the group in the possession of positionally distributed goods is bad for the envier." [169] Hence, an individual can be envious of the superior position of a group of which he is not a member. This might be "the rich," "the privileged," "Wall Street," or some other congregation that the envier perceives has an unfair share of such "positionally distributed goods."

Progressives themselves make it a point to assign collective emotions to what they refer to as identity groups," making collective emotional generalizations of "white guilt," "white rage," "white fragility" (and now even "brown fragility" in a seeming hierarchy of skin color) in course of promoting what most refer to as *identity politics*. They ascribe emotions like fear and phobias to non-Progressive groups based on the latter's opposing worldview, sex, perceived sexual preferences, or economic status: classes of people that Progressives routinely accuse of homophobia, xenophobia, or simply in fear of losing what the Progressive perceives as their "colonial hegemony," "privilege," or "patriarchy

Like a corporation, community, or a nation, social movements can develop their culture or "psyche" – one that mirrors the psychological makeup of the majority of its members or active supporters. This includes the prominent emotions that motivate them to passively or actively support the movement in the first instance. For example, envy has been demonstrated to be a potential motivator among government agency decision-makers.[170] Agencies can be driven by envious motives when establishing agency plans and goals. Envy of other government agencies that have comparably related mission focus – i.e., where there is a perceived gap in some desirable function, like responsibility for and control over law and regulation creation, intelligence collection, or national defense.[171] If similar emotions are the political motivators for a significant number of individuals who make up a social or revolutionary movement, then they can and should be considered, as Jung pointed out, as the "psychopathology of the masses," i.e., as determinative of the movement's "psyche" or culture.

Americans increasingly use words like "mass psychosis" when trying to decipher and describe the collective beliefs and actions of the modern Progressive Movement. And the word *psychosis* does refer to certain conditions that affect the mind, specifically "where there has been some loss of contact with reality." That is, indicators of a psychosis include delusions, incoherent or nonsensical speech, and acting out in a way that is totally inappropriate for a given situation. In general, the Progressive Movement's members and supporters, those who are grown adults, do seem to exhibit these symptoms. Many of their affirmations of what they consider factual, for example, that human males can have and breastfeed babies (a/k/a "chest feed"), are seriously delusional. That female swimmers can fairly compete with male swimmers is similarly so. Their sincere self-diagnosis of suffering from a "derangement syndrome" after the 2016 elections, demonstrates a serious emotional fragility in many of their ranks which is a healthy mind would be a response impossible to comprehend. Their fear of any political speech contrary to Progressive ideology and for which they require the emotional protection of safe spaces. That a person's identity is not the sum of his or her personality and character traits but consists of how many "identity groups" with whom they can associate. That nothing can be proven to be true, and that highways and even charitable donating are racist. Their cries for defunding police agencies in high crime areas where they are needed most and their support for economic programs that have been proven time and again to be detrimental to an economy – one of the most important indicators of a functioning and healthy society. Not least of all is the Progressive's demonstrated zealotry – always a harbinger of potential irrational social and political behavior – in their support for their various platforms and goals and their quick and severe reactions to others' contradictory ideas. That these issues are fundamentally social and political seems to be the only indicator in favor of ruling out a psychosis in the individual Progressive. However, as for the psyche of the Movement *en masse*, it is not a wholly inaccurate characterization.

The Movement has also increasingly been viewed as akin to a religion. This too is not far off the mark, and there are many similarities between it and religion. For example, guilt can serve as an effective source of a social movement's unity by fostering "a poignant sense of sin" – one that requires "an act of atonement" that, of course, serves the movement.[172] For the modern Progressive Movement, this sense of sin is obviously satisfied by the pervasive sense of "guilt" in its members. Guilt for being white, "feeling guilty for slavery," guilt for being rich and not paying their "fair share," or simply for having too much "white privilege." They feel guilty for having believed before they became "woke" that men in bras and breastfeeding were not normal. By being "woke" the Progressive mimics the "born again" Christian who finally accepts Jesus as Savior, the final step in renouncing original sin and receiving the power of righteousness. Being "woke," they now see the inherent injustice about them, and they have the power of "social justice" and a movement behind them. Similarly, a Socialist Collective society living in a world free from "colonial oppression," heteronormativity, patriarchy, the conceptual nuclear family, no private property and thus no crime, no police, open borders, etc. – this is the Progressive's Promised Land. This is Utopia and is, in essence, the equivalent of Heaven in the Progressive Movement ideology. And if Utopia is heaven, then Hell is Climate Change. To reach Utopian heaven and avoid the peril of Climate hell, the Progressive must self-sacrifice now, including and specifically his freedom for conformity. Symbols of worship, like a rainbow or ANTIFA flag, a rehashed Hammer and Sickle – for the Progressive these are religious symbols akin to Christianity's Cross or Islam's Crescent. Finally, like some who are compelled to zealotry through their religious beliefs, so too are there many in the Progressive Movement who engage in similar zealotry in the advocacy of their socio-political ideology and to the point of violence, destruction, and murder.

There is little question that envy is an emotional player in the American Progressive's psychology sufficiently present in its members that it could be considered as a defining characteristic of the Progressive Movement's "group psyche." This can be seen repeatedly in Progressive social media posts and conversations, as well as Progressive leaning articles that target individual wealth accumulation, private ownership of property, etc.: the Economist's outlandish article that private property is undermining capitalism, the Boston Globe reporter's fascination with the salaries of "high powered" attorneys, investors, and family incomes that she and others "can only dream about," the New York Times contributor's ramblings about the "rich flipping their shit." The Progressives' envy of those financially better off than them is consistently present, even though there is no outright admission of it. It is the first of the "common symptoms" of the individual that Jung believed could be used to examine the psychopathy of the analogous mass phenomena. This is the fundamental basis for ultimate control over the production, wealth, status, and other "positionally distributed goods" through higher income taxation, wealth taxation, nationalization, and other means of redistribution. It is not, as the Toronto study found, out of a sense of "fairness," but simply self-interest and envy. For the Progressive, the envy emotion subconsciously helps drive them toward their final Collectivist state, but at the same time, they loudly profess that the ridding of envy generally will be one of the *results* of the Collectivist State.

As with envy, indefinite fear appears a consistent preoccupation of the American Progressive. It is the Progressive Movement's collective fear of freedom, of the true liberty that it perceives as threats to them as individuals since without Collective governmental support they would "starve on the street," lose the Climate Change war, or at least be unable to "create art."[173] Progressives, in fact, harbor a distinct disdain for self-reliance because by definition it flies in the face of Collectivism and, for the Critical Race proponents, relying on oneself is strictly an aspect of "whiteness." For those who fear the potential consequences of the liberty and freedom inherent in Capitalist systems, or who are envious of those who 'do better' under capitalist norms, Socialism provides the notion that emotional relief is possible "to rest, to rest, to rest," or at least "not to starve to death." The Collective will take care of everyone, and it will do that which is "good for everyone." There is, after all, safety in numbers and if the collective includes everyone then how can we all not be safe. Indefinite fear is thus susceptible to individual dependency on government and dependency fosters power and control over the individual, one further step toward subservience to the Collective.

Finally, for many white Progressives "guilt" takes center stage in seeking their identity and reason to exist. Feeling guilty for having caused and or perpetuated systemically racist institutions through, for example, patriarchy and colonialism, his masochistic urges can be satisfied, rewarded in knowing that he is being punished for his racism and "implicit biases." And guilt is also a means of control used to convince would-be Progressives that their only salvation for their wrongful acts and thoughts is to become an anti-racist or a "social justice warrior." Not least of all, teaching school children that they are citizens of a country that is "inherently racist, xenophobic, misogynist," – i.e., evil, has a strong possibility to create a feeling of self-loathing, self-defeat, and ultimately masochistic behavior – life-long behavior that is self-destructive, although it may further the Progressive Movement's recruitment.

Like JEM, who satisfied her masochistic urge to suffer for her self-diagnosed (and misdiagnosed) racism by her submission to the antiracist movement–her Thing–JEM felt the righteous authority of the Thing. This emotional connection was sufficient to cause her to believe that she needed to control her target–the outspoken public school mother–by trying to get her fired from her job. In social media post screenshots captured as evidence in the civil court case against her, JEM appeared to revel in the praise that she received from other apparently Progressive "friends" in an "Equity" Facebook Group. As they cheered her on for her efforts to have the school mother fired from her employment, JEM appeared to take on the character of the martyr, making bold and righteous sounding statements to the effect that she would *never back down from the fight*, and (not uncommon in depressive personality disorders) made paranoid projections that it was actually *the mother who was 'bullying' her* by filing a lawsuit to stop her from contacting the mother's employer. JEM was now the minor sadist with the righteous authority of the antiracist movement behind her, setting out to control and inflict emotional distress on a local mother in one instance, and to get another private citizen speaking out against Defund the Police fired in another instance.

And the minor sadist is simply a bully. It's this bullying behavior that Americans recognize most in the outward character and personality of many modern Progressives: that they are just bullies loud, obnoxious, and belligerent in their actions and their words. They will bully anyone arguing against their ideal of control and, with little encouraging, will go after reputations, jobs, and seemingly more frequently, encourage physical assault and worse.

Tolerate No Rival

Sadism – in whatever form – is all about power and control over another. Social control is the major, massive premise of both Fascist and Communist Collectivism. "Both the sadistic and masochistic trends," wrote Fromm, "are caused by the inability of the isolated individual to stand alone and his need for a symbiotic relationship that overcomes this aloneness." [174] To willingly submit to complete control, and then to eventually come to be part of the controlling authority, satisfies many of the "deep psychic needs" of the majority Progressive supporters – their faux guilt, their fear of the indefinite, and their envy of those around them who they believe have more than they do. True freedom seems a hostile wilderness for many Progressives who fear its heavy set of responsibilities and potential consequences.

Through both their individual acts and the Movement's ideology and platforms, Progressives consistently demonstrate an obvious deep desire for total power, control, and forceful submission to their ideology: over the population, education, students, parents, the economy, consumers, producers, prices, wages, gender, demographics, the global climate, and speech to name just a few. But to arise and to persist, both Fascism and Communism require one-party rule. As Hitler recognized in his plan to establish sole rule of the Nazi Party, those who are not comfortable with freedom and liberty, "are far more satisfied by a doctrine which tolerates no rival..." To bring about Fascism in the United States, American Progressives are actively seeking to disrupt or replace long-standing institutions that all but guarantee that one-party rule will not develop. The first is the U.S. Constitution which they criticize in vague terms like racist, misogynist, or simply just "too old." Failing that, their more immediate concern has been the Constitutional provision calling for an electoral college, and the First Amendment's protection of the right to free speech.

As has been recognized since the beginning of the human social conflict, the pen is, ultimately, mightier than the sword. Whether, pen, printing press, or social media, the American Progressive is scared to death of free speech. Beginning in earnest in the 1980s with "political correctness," *shadow banning, fact-checking,* and other terms have relatively recently come to describe censorship of conservative speech on social media platforms – speech that Progressives equate with "violence" or "dangerous," expanding the need for safe spaces to protect their emotional fragility. Attacking the conservative speaker rather than his or her argument is a favorite tactic and effective when the intended audience cannot understand the difference.

Labeling one's opponent as a homophobe or racist can do wonders when avoiding the tougher questions. Controlling speech is emotionally satisfying to both the Progressive's masochistic as well as sadistic urges: "Rather than controlling people's bodies with guns, they control their minds with… politically correct epithets. It's much more satisfying to be able to claim that anything your opponent is saying is racist…It's a much greater exercise of power." [175]

Many who claim to be emotionally uncomfortable or feel "threatened" by another's discourse on issues of freedom and liberty, or who have been led to believe that speech is "violence" (or that "silence is violence" – take your pick) are convinced that the government has an obligation to protect *them* from those with rival viewpoints. It is they who have the superior "right" to have another's speech squelched. As of this writing, the current Progressive administration has created a Federal "Disinformation Governance Board" charged with detecting and determining what is or isn't truthful information across a range of media platforms. Although outright censorship may prove to be tough given the protections in the First Amendment, the thought of one federal government official or agency making labeling another's speech as "disinformation" is a step toward greater control. Countering government Board censorship through the courts, should it occur, would be a long, uphill battle even though victory was in the end a sure thing – which it never is in any litigation.

The objective of controlling speech, of course, is to set the Progressive narrative and further their goal of one-party rule and ultimately Socialist Fascism. Banning "disinformation" through government or private action, meanwhile, makes it much easier to promote the destruction of another impediment to one-party Socialist rule: the electoral college.

The Framers of the Constitution understood the nature of power, and the danger of one person or body having a monopoly on it. They all knew that "power corrupts" and if concentrated in only one or a few hands, power would more likely than not lead to authoritarian, dictatorial rule. Although it took several years of debate, the Framers adopted the "Separation of Powers" concept coined by the 18th-century philosopher Montesquieu, creating different branches of government that could "check and balance" the acts of the other.[176] These branches would form a single central government, itself with limited authority and power, to govern the various states. The people of states, on the other hand, would elect and send their own representatives – a set number based on the total population of the state– to compose the first branch, the Congress.[177] In order to elect a president, each state would choose and send to the capital representatives equal in number to their state representatives and who would cast their vote in favor of one or another candidate as the people so chose. This was to help ensure that it was not a simple "majority vote," i.e., the popular vote, that would determine the office of president. This was one protection so presciently included in the Constitution to help prevent a "tyranny of the majority" – the equivalent of one-party rule. In today's terms, were it not for the process of the electoral college, more than likely those states with megacities like New York, Los Angeles, and Chicago, would be consistently choosing one branch of the government while having large blocs in the Congress, and thus dictating to the other states who would have little to no say in federal governance? And for that reason, Progressives have waged a campaign to discredit it. "I think it needs to be eliminated," Progressive icon Hillary Clinton told CNN, "I'd like to see us move beyond it, yes."[178] This was, of course, after she lost the 2016 election even though taking the popular vote.

Open Borders and National Suicide

As Horney, Fromm, De Beauvoir, and others realized masochistic urges that begin to overwhelm the individual seek as their end the "extinction of the individual self"–the spiritual merger with a dominant object in order to share in its superior power. Fascism and Communism, in their drive to extinguish the individual within the Collective, are a drive with a simultaneous "lust for power and suicide."[179] Such a masochistic lust can be observed today in the actions and platforms of the Congressional Progressive Caucus that reflect the Progressive Movement's ideology, as well as in the actions (and lack of required action) of the self-described "most Progressive President in history," Joe Biden.[180] At the time of writing, it is clear that Biden is advised by Progressives within his administration who share the masochistic desire not only for one-party, authoritarian rule, but also what could be considered the suicidal end to the United States as a nation, to wit: their "open borders" policy.

This suicidal urge is clear in the current Progressive administration's policy regarding the U.S. southern border. As soon as "the most progressive president in history" took office, the number of immigrants entering illegally rose dramatically. His campaign promises as well as his actions once in office ignited a crisis, which his administration has completely ignored and clearly with the intent to consider the U.S. southern border as a non-existent boundary. Since the spring of 2021, the U.S. has been inundated with numbers of immigrants entering without inspection, not only from Latin American countries, but from all over the world – including many who have known associations with terrorism, child sex trafficking, murder, and associations with transnational criminal organizations, just for starters. While many of these criminals who cross illegally into the United States are fortuitously caught by the U.S. Border Patrol, many are not. They enter our nation without any trace of their presence, their whereabouts, or their intent.

Erasing a national border is akin to national suicide, and the most Progressive administration ever is engaging in this "extinction" of the nation in an ironic lust for more power *over* the nation. That is, they are taking no serious action to defend our borders and thus protect United States citizens because they believe, as many political scientists have pointed out, that newly arriving illegal aliens will one day soon be awarded a permanent residency and then citizenship. Once that happens, their theory goes, political demographics will change dramatically in favor of the Democrat Party and therefore Progressive platforms. This will finally deliver them the one-party rule necessary to finally realize Socialist Utopia.

This behavior of the Progressive Movement fits squarely within the description of the sadomasochistic urge. That is, to commit national suicide to acquire more power over the nation and its direction. This same urge can be seen in the Progressive mantras that all American institutions must be destroyed and replaced because they are inherently racist, oppressive, misogynist, and so forth. The destruction of institutions, like legal reasoning and the Constitution that were created on universal, objective, and neutral, premises (what Progressive scholars consider "colonialist" or "male" values) is again a sign of the masochistic urge to destroy the foundation of what is by any objective standard the freest nation in human history. That is, the Movement that has the right to exist because of the freedom that those values have created is intent on destroying those values and resultant freedom. Similarly, the Movement's urge to be part of that destruction is simultaneous with the sadistic urge to be a part of whatever is to emerge from the destruction – be it a new national order or the, even more powerful, a new world order.

Instead of one having to submit herself unconditionally to her nation in order to defend it from those intent on destroying it, the new fascism that the American Progressive desires are within the context of Globalism. It is not the nation or its people that are the important thing for the new Fascist, but the world. In typical masochistic delusion, the modern Progressive believes she is saving the existence of the nation by erasing its borders to ensure its nonexistence. In their sadistic craving for power over the nation's people, the Movement will cede the nation's power on the global stage to be at the will of powerful others.

To finally succeed, however, the Progressive Movement must overcome the Constitution, and it must have more power in numbers, in popular support which will provide them more like-minded representatives in government – numbers that it hopes to attain by overloading demographics with illegal immigration well beyond what Congress presently authorizes annually through legal immigration. Through this, it sees a huge opportunity to change American culture and values, from Individualism, self-reliance, and freedom, to total dependence and thus subservience to the Collective.

But Progressives also recognize a potential source of power already here at home.

Primary and Secondary Public Education

Children are naturally very susceptible to influence, not only by their peers but even more so by adult role models. This is especially true as they go through the stages of developing their individual identities during adolescence. Adults naturally can have an impact on a child's emotional development and informing moral beliefs and, because their minds are still developing, adults can easily convince children to believe something that, in fact, is not true. For example, and as mentioned earlier, one exception to the requirement that a person actually is responsible for the injurious act that evokes the guilt emotion is in the case of young children and adolescents. Children can easily be convinced that they have done something injurious to others, and a true feeling of guilt can arise if the child believes this to be so. Similarly, and in a relevant part, they can also be led to believe that a recognized mental disorder – such as *gender dysphoria* – is part of the normal human condition. Adolescents may tend – as adolescents often do – to believe that this dysphoria is actually something desirable, convincing themselves that they suffer from it along with those young people (and adults) who truly do struggle with it.

Since 1917 Socialists, whether Nationalist Fascists or Communists, have realized the impressionable nature of youth, and during or after every revolution have attempted to wrest control of education. Probably because of its inherent contradictions, it is much easier to convince a child of Socialism's virtues than it is to convince an experienced adult, at least without using violence and mental coercion. "Experience," as Eric Hoffman noted in his discourse on mass movements, "is a handicap" to a movement that is made up of those totally ignorant of what they seek. It is simply easier to recruit inexperienced youth to support a movement, and they often make for excellent zealots. Cubans after Castro's Communist revolution there woke up to this when the government created schools for their children in the *campo*, physically distant from their homes, and where the new ruling Socialists could instill the revolutionary spirit in them without interference. When parents did try to interfere, even just attempting to check on their children, many were convicted of crimes and interned.[181] Similarly, Hitler's National Socialists also attempted to control primary and secondary education, professing that the German students "entire education and development have to be directed at giving him the conviction of being absolutely superior to the others."[182] Other Soviet satellite or Socialist nations in the Twentieth Century had their Socialist youth groups, for example, the former People's Republic of Yugoslavia's "Young Pioneers."

Today, one can see an effort at similar control and indoctrination by many Progressive public-school teachers and boards of education. This is particularly true in the areas of "social justice," "racial justice," "Collectivist pedagogy," and other theories with origins in Marxist ideology. They believe that it is necessary to teach various tenants of critical theories to their pupils for the latter's social and emotional welfare. Progressive activist teachers believe that white students should be forced to accept that they are "oppressors" because of the color of their skin, and that minority students are inescapably victims of that oppression for the same reason. The authoritarian educator demands of children that they accept, without rebellion, that they are in one or the other of these race or identity classes. Others, like Gipe, coerce them through vague explanations of "feeling uncomfortable" and awarding extra credit to attend political rallies in order to "turn them into revolutionaries."

Beginning in and around 2020, various local, state, and national teachers' unions began to exhibit a clear, overwhelmingly strong urge for complete control in the emotional development of school children. [183] Specifically, unions, as well as some "parent organizations" that support both critical race theory and transgenderism, have tried to wrest control from parents the responsibility of instilling moral and ethical values in their children. Often referring to public school students as "*my* children," Progressive-minded teachers in kindergarten through twelfth grade ("K-12") believe that they are the only ones capable of accomplishing this. Most notably by promoting the ideas inherent to critical race theory and Marxist social justice, as well as human sexuality and gender. *Not* being permitted to do this, they believe, is a violation of *their rights* – rights they seem to believe are superior to a parent's or guardian's natural or legal rights as either the biological or legal guardians of their children.

What Progressives underestimated was the primacy and strength of the parent-child relationship – one that can be said to share no greater love. When parents in some school systems, not only the larger urban systems but also many rural districts, began to understand the depth of the indoctrination of their children in collectivism vis a vis "equity," "intersectionalism," "racial justice" and related critical concepts, many became very vocal. Others saw the fundamentally twisted Progressive imperative that kindergartners and elementary school kids must be taught about transgenderism and sexual identity at an age where any reasonable person knows they would never understand it and while the American education system, in general, was producing less and less academically competitive adults. These notions, as well as the backlash, cut across any racial or socio-economic divides.

Parents appeared at local school board meetings, often irate and vehemently chastising and challenging the local board members. Videos began to go viral showing parents lambasting school boards for not only allowing but in some cases actively promoting – knowingly or unknowingly–collectivist ideas. At times, the police would be called in and parents escorted out of the meetings. When parents began to call out teachers and teachers unions, the unions doubled down on the primacy of their control and "responsibility" for the social and emotional development of children over that of the parents. The world would never reach its Utopian potential, they seemed to say if parents were allowed to have a say in the social and emotional learning of their children.

By early 2021, teachers and parents who supported critical race theory and teaching transgenderism to very young children, began to retaliate and use typical Progressive tactics. In Loudoun County, Virginia, a county that would take center stage in the emerging public education debate, "[a]private Facebook group made up of Virginia parents, teachers, and school board members…reportedly target[ed] parents opposed to critical race theory…" The group called itself "anti-racist parents of Loudoun County" and had several hundred members.[184] Like JEM, their intent was to target parents opposed to teaching concepts inherent in Critical Race Theory. And like her, their modus operandi was to "infiltrate," "hack," and otherwise "expose" those parents, not least of all to the latter's employers, with the intent to silence them. Fascism can tolerate no rival.

On September 29th, 2021, after several months of seeming tumultuous school board meetings, the National Association of School Boards (NASB) president, Viola Garcia, in an unprecedented and overly dramatic action, notified the President of the United States that his *"immediate assistance is required to protect our students, school board members, and educators..."* Citing news clips and articles about upset elementary and high school parents acting rudely at school board meetings, Garcia suggested that the Department of Homeland Security, the FBI's *"National Security Branch and its Counterterrorism Division,"* needed to deploy into school districts around the country. Irate parents, she argued, were engaging boards of education in a way that *"could be the equivalent to a form of domestic terrorism and hate crimes."* In a very over-eager reception, which immediately caused suspicion among many observers and members of Congress, the Department of Justice and Attorney General Merrick Garland took action, creating an alliance between Federal law enforcement agencies and resources and local community policing to monitor and report on parents.[185]

In many school districts across the country, teachers are now subjected to professional development that includes training in "Collectivism" sometimes using books and manuals that use and promote the term, but never define it.[186] In a Maryland school district, a superintendent of schools was confronted with these facts by an elected board of education member. The superintendent argued that collectivism doesn't really mean *collectivism* "when used in pedagogy." This appeared, however, suspect since she was unable to produce another definition for it in the context of pedagogy. In the professional development course, teachers were informed that the United States was one of the nations that emphasized Individualism and that we needed to become "more Collectivist." The professional development thus appeared to be an attempt to inculcate a subtle acceptance of the notion of Collectivism as something socially innocuous and socially desirable but without defining it.

The urge to prompt revolutionary thoughts in young people is not restricted to the classroom as Progressive activists work in other areas besides formal education. The popular magazine Teen Vogue has sought to influence adolescent readers to believe that the United States Constitution is outdated, outmoded, and racist: that "we need a new one." In an age-appropriate article titled "The U.S. Needs a New Constitution," the Teen Vogue author argues that "the United States should replace its constitution with one guided by principles of equality and human rights."[187] She argues that our Constitution is the oldest still in use in the world and that almost every other country has "modernized" theirs (omitting, of course, that for many countries this was after a coup d'etat or other violent regime change that threw the last constitution out the window, the new constitution awaiting a similar fate as soon as the next regime change comes around).

In another Teen Vogue article, the author enlists the help of two child stage actors, "RC" and "TW" both African Americans, asking them, "[w]hat's a problem with our current Constitution that you'd like to see fixed? Their response, which one would expect from a thirteen-year-old, and which shows the author's exploitation of these youth to satisfy her own political viewpoint:

RC: I think that our Constitution is a rough draft and we can do better. I googled the Constitution and I tried to read it. I kept scrolling, scrolling, and scrolling. I'm just like, 'Can I get some real language here?' I feel like it's way too convoluted and we can fix that. First of all, to get people to actually try to understand it. There are many amendments that we can add or modify, like the Equal Rights Amendment. Our show's motto, 'We all belong in the preamble,' I think we should add that.

TW: *'We the people' is in the preamble — it's just the definition of it isn't good enough.*

RC: *Exactly. That's why I think we can change that.*

TW: *But what are they gonna say? We the African-American people, the white people, like —*

RC: *I don't know! [Laughs] I'm not a — we could probably say something like 'all of us' or...*

TW: *That's vague, that's ambiguous."* [188]

The demonstrated urge by many local and national teachers' unions to strip parents and guardians of the control over what their children are taught is indicative of the sadist urge, not only to control the children but to control the child's parents as well. There is also another consequence to Cultural Marxist theories to the young; one that potentially has long-lasting psychological consequences. That is, by disingenuously teaching impressionable children that they are racist oppressors, victims of racism, or citizens of a racist country that was "founded on racism," Progressives are setting children up for self-hate and self-defeat. In short, for a life of moral masochism and self-defeating, if not ultimately self-destructive, urges and behavior.

That children are a target of American Progressives who seek to implement the tenets of critical theories and Marxism is, at least since 2020, beyond question and frankly not surprising. After all, "[w]e must hate," Lenin said in his 1923 speech to the Russian Commissars of Education, "hatred is the basis of Communism. Children must be taught to hate their parents if they are not Communists."[189] For the Progressive Movement bent on the suicide of the nation, the shining path lay through hatred of America and division of its population through "identity politics." And if hatred is to be instilled at the expense of education, logic, and universal "colonial" values such as objectivity and reason, then so much the better says the Progressive: the young will learn to become dependent on the Collective and less self-reliant.

A Short Conclusion

"What could be more absurd than to suppose the same ignorant and common people you despise, when taken one by one, are of any greater consequence when taken together?"

– **Cicero**

The emotional American Progressive is, like Schoeck's *envious man*, "Inevitably a disturber of the peace, a potential saboteur, an instigator of mutiny and, fundamentally, he cannot be placated by others."[190] It is evident in the political and social rhetoric, reasoning, and acts of the American Progressive, that he or she is prone to act upon one, if not a combination, of several powerful emotions: envy, fear, and/or guilt. Each of these, by themselves or in combination and when experienced chronically, can result in destructive or debilitating behavior in the individual and can prompt masochistic and thus sadist urges deep within. These urges manifest themselves behaviorally in various ways, including through moral masochism: a faux egalitarian concern dressed as legitimate "concern for moral justice." Like the one who would prefer to penalize one wealthier than him in order to fund a social program that he knows will only hurt those it was intended to help, the moral masochist is always in touch with his sadistic urge to control and harm.

There exists a symbiotic relationship between the Progressive masochist who, in order to quell his fragile emotions, so desires to become subservient to some powerful Thing, and the Progressive sadist who is more than willing to provide an authoritarian cause to satisfy the need. The modern American Progressive Movement is characterized by this Social Sadomasochism. Progressive ideology demands one-party rule and social conformity to its platforms, from wealth redistribution to national pro-choice policies. The majority of its supporters, including many Democrats, are eager to live in a one-party, homogenous state with a government that will ultimately control nearly every facet of their existence, and they will not hesitate to enforce whatever platform the Government promulgates – from mandatory experimental vaccination and masking to land reform if it is only sold as good for the Collective.

Viewing the acts of individual Progressives and the Progressive Movement itself through a sadomasochistic lens – the ultimate mental state of the totalitarian–is a critical component toward deciphering the psychological motivations behind Progressive philosophy, its platforms, and thus its appeal to those who overly rely on emotion rather than experience and logic in their political decision-making. It is also critical to understand how to counter Progressivism's drive toward social and national suicide. The Social Sadomasochistic urge, if not recognized and checked but allowed to continue its current trajectory unchallenged through democratic processes, is likely to lead the United States – and by default, the world – into fascism that will make the destruction, death, and torture of the Twentieth Century look like child's play.

The Collective's "equity" platform–the keystone inherent to Marxist Socialism–is no new paradigm, and although many Progressives seem to believe they are tapping into some novel and powerful social doctrine, they are all still thinking inside what is just a worn-out box. Couched as "neo-Marxism," "Cultural Marxism," or "critical theory," history has shown time and again that Socialist Collectivism has never worked as intended. It has consistently resulted in unparalleled mediocracy, misery, destruction, and death. Like all the past failed schemes of equitable distribution of resources in world history, modern Progressive Marxist ideology is based on the flawed premise that men and women do not act in their own self-interests. It is a faulty premise that has consistently plagued Marxist theory and its revolutionaries, and it continues to confound the modern American Progressive even today. Through its failures, it is a theory that has always prompted Authoritarianism – Fascist or Communist – with the power for violence directed at those who will not conform to its fallacy.

True freedom can only be experienced by an individual, as only the loss of that freedom can. Today, individual freedom is being stripped from Americans by an American Progressive Movement whose supporters engage in acts of violent intimidation, which they see as righteous. There is an obvious fanatical attachment of Progressives to Socialist and one-party Fascist political practices, the power of which Americans must not underestimate or ignore. As Fromm poignantly noted in 1941 about Nazi Fascism, part of German society "was deeply attracted to the new ideology and fanatically attached to those who proclaimed it." [191] However, its success also counted on the other part of the population, those who "bowed to the Nazi regime without any strong resistance, but also without becoming admirers of the Nazi ideology and political practice."[192]

155

Americans of all walks of life who value Individualism, freedom, and self-reliance have now more than ever an individual responsibility to arrest the fanatical drive toward Socialist Fascism; to get out of the defensive mode and take back the offensive from Progressives and their Movement. Not emotionally prone to political zealotry like those of the Progressive Left, freedom-loving Americans have only recently rediscovered their power and their own strong voices able to articulate their values – values that those of the Progressive Left in their hypocrisy and chronic contradiction cannot rival. Bowing to the Movement without resistance will only result in a similar national suicide as was visited upon the German people under Nationalist Socialist rule. Standing up to and refusing to be bullied by social sadists intent on seeing Americans bow in submission to the Collective – that amorphous body that has no soul, no sound reasoning, and which is capable only of ignorant mob justice in its suicidal urge to divide us as a nation. Teaching children to beware of teachers who are preaching divisiveness to become self-reliant and to learn its virtues both for the community and nation, but also as a way to live life with as much freedom and liberty as possible, and to preserve it for others. Running for political office, from school boards to state executives, and exposing the fascistic, sadomasochistic tendencies of the American Progressive Movement at every opportunity.

Freedom-loving Americans are, through their traditional community values, persistence, self-reliance, and determination, coming together and realizing the irrational and emotional instability of American Progressives and their Movement and its dangers. Americans must also realize that many Progressive Movement supporters have no idea of the Marxist origins of its ideology, the Marxist ideology in its political platforms, and the tendency that Marxism has for authoritarianism and totalitarianism. At every opportunity, those who might serve as fodder for the Progressive Movement's destructive tendencies need to be educated on its origins.

Not least of all, we need to show others that we do not fear the base acts and destructive actions of which Progressives are demonstrably capable – from their petty bullying to their attacks on livelihoods or reputations, to physical threats. For Americans who value freedom, the Progressive activist is no one to fear–as Cicero said of the ignorant several thousand years ago–neither individually nor collectively.

Bibliography

Abraham, Victoria. "The U.S. Needs a New Constitution to Address the Fundamental Wrong of Slavery." Teen Vogue. June 3, 2021. https://www.teenvogue.com/story/united-states-needs-new-constitution.

Adams, Becket. "Seven Months Later, 1619 Project Leader Admits She Got it Wrong." Washington Examiner, March 12, 2020. https://www.washingtonexaminer.com/opinion/seven-months-later-1619-project-leader-admits-she-got-it-wrong?msclkid=9dc787c4cee411ec-94745627d5ca0cf4.

American Psychiatric Association. Diagnostic and Statistical Manual of Mental Disorders. Washington D.C.: American Psychiatric Association. 1994.

Ashback, Charles, PhD. "Persecutory Objects, Guilt and Shame." Self Hatred in Psychoanalysis, Brunner-Routledge (2003). Scharff and Tsigounis, Eds.

Barakat, Matthew. "School System Pulls 2 Books with Graphic Sex from Libraries." ABC News, September 24, 2021. https://abcnews.go.com/Entertainment/wireStory/school-system-pulls-books-graphic-sex-libraries-80219516.

Ben-Ze'ev, Aaron. "Envy and Inequality." Journal of Philosophy 89, no. 11 (November 1992): 551-581. https://doi.org/10.2307/2941056.

Bender, Leslie. "A Lawyer's Primer on Feminist Theory and Tort." Journal of Legal Education 38, No. 1 (March/June 1988): 3 – 37.

Bernstein, Richard. Dictatorship of Virtue. New York: Knopf, Inc. 1994.

Bois, Paul. "New York Times Contributor Sarah Jeong: Inflation Hysteria 'Driven by Rich People Flipping Their S***'" Breitbart News. November 18, 2021. https://www.breitbart.com/economy/2021/11/18/new-york-times-contributor-sarah-jeong-inflation-hysteria-driven-by-rich-people-flipping-their-s/.

Bresenahan, John, Kyle Cheney. "Bizarre Fight Breaks out in House over Whether Socialists are Nazis." Politico, March 26, 2019. https://www.politico.com/story/2019/03/26/congress-socialist-nazi-debate-1237472.

Chak, Avinash. "Beyond 'He' and 'She': The Rise of Non-Binary Pronouns." BBC, December 7, 2015. https://www.bbc.com/news/magazine-34901704.

Chillizza, Chris. "Sorry, Hillary Clinton. The Electoral College Isn't Going Anywhere." CNN, September 14, 2017. https://www.cnn.com/2017/09/14/politics/electoral-college/index.html.

Christie, George C., and Patrick H. Martin. Jurisprudence. St. Paul: West Group. 1995.

De Beauvoir, Simone. The Ethics of Ambiguity. New York: Open Road Integrated Media. 2018.

De Quevedo, Francisco, and R. K. Britton. Dreams and Discourses. Liverpool: Liverpool University Press. 1989. https://www.liverpooluniversitypress.co.uk/books/id/54108/

Delumeau, Jean. *Sin and Fear*. New York: St. Martin's Press. 1990. Eric Nicholson translation.

DeVega, Chauncey. "Dear Joe Biden: We Don't Want 'Unity' with Fascists — That's Why Democrats Lose." Salon Magazine, March 4, 2022. https://www.salon.com/2022/03/04/dear-joe-biden-seeking-unity-with-the-fascists-is-exactly-why-democrats-lose/.

Dorman, Sam. "PBS Station Defends Drag Queen Skit for Kids: 'Performance Art That Can Inspire Creative Thinking.'" Fox News, May 20, 2021. https://www.foxnews.com/us/pbs-station-defends-drag-queen-kids.

Duffy, Michelle K., Kristin L. Scott, Jason D. Shaw, Bennett J. Tepper and Karl Aquino. "A Social Context Model of Envy and Social Undermining." Academy of Management Journal 55, No. 3 (8 Sep 2012): https://doi.org/10.5465/amj.2009.0804.

Durkheim, Emile. The Rule of Sociological Method. New York: Free Press. 2013.

Editors, Economist Magazine. "Home Ownership is the West's Biggest Economic-Policy Mistake. It is an Obsession that Undermines Growth, Fairness, and Public Faith in Capitalism." The Economist, January 16, 2020. https://www.economist.com/leaders/2020/01/16/home-owner-ship-is-the-wests-biggest-economic-policy-mistake.

Evans, Bergen. Dictionary of Quotations. New York: Bonanza Books. 1968.

Farnsworth, Ward. The Practicing Stoic. Boston: David R. Godine. 2019.

Faulkner, Harold U. The Quest of Social Justice 1898–1914. Chicago: Quadrangle Book. 1971.

Fearnow, Benjamin. "Joe Biden Says He'd Be the 'Most Progressive' President in History, Tells Bernie Sanders to 'Disown' Misogynistic Supporters." Newsweek, February 16, 2020. https://www.newsweek.com/joe-biden-says-hed-most-progressive-president-history-tells-bernie-sanders-disown-1487567.

Freud, Sigmund. The Ego and the Id. New Delhi: General Press. 2020.

Fromm, Erich. Escape From Freedom. New York: Henry Holt and Co. 1994.

Fromm, Erich. Marx's Concept of Man. Connecticut: Martino Publishing. 2011.

Garcia, Marcela. "Why the Rich Should Pay More in Taxes." Boston Globe, May 28, 2021. https://www.bostonglobe.com/2021/05/28/opinion/why-rich-should-pay-more/.

Graham, John R. "The Constitution and Your 'Right to Health Care.'" National Review, June 9, 2010. https://www.nationalreview.com/critical-condition/constitution-and-your-right-health-care-john-r-graham/.

Hammond, Zaretta. Culturally Responsive Teaching and the Brain, 1st edition. California: Corwin. 2014.

Hawkins, Kristan. "Remove Statues of Margaret Sanger, Planned Parenthood Founder Tied to Eugenics and Racism." USA Today, July 23, 2020. https://www.usatoday.com/story/opinion/2020/07/23/racism-eugenics-margaret-sanger-deserves-no-honors-column/5480192002/.

Hill Collins, Patricia, and Sirma Bilge. Intersectionality (Key Concepts), 2nd Edition. Wiley and Sons, Inc. Kindle.

Hitler, Adolf. Mein Kampf. Boston: Houghton Mifflin, 1999.

Hoffer, Eric. The True Believer. New York: Harper Perennial. 2010.

Johnston, Victor S. Why We Feel. New York: Perseus Books. 1999.

Jones, Kipp. "Georgetown Students Reportedly Request Place to 'Cry' as Dean Addresses Ilya Shapiro's SCOTUS Tweets." MSM, February 1, 2022. https://www.msn.com/en-us/news/us/georgetown-students-reportedly-request-place-to-cry-as-dean-addresses-ilya-shapiro-s-scotus-tweets/ar-AATnrMC.

Judicial Watch. "Montgomery County Schools Teacher Training Records Show Lessons on 'Restorative Justice' and 'Psychoeducation.'" November 4, 2021. https://www.judicialwatch.org/montgomery-schools-crt/

Jung, Carl G. Modern Man in Search of a Soul. New York: Harcourt, Inc. 1993.

Kotkin, Joel. "The Most Dangerous Class. The Coming Revenge of the Disappointed." National Review, March 29, 2022. https://www.nationalreview.com/2022/03/the-most-dangerous-class/?utm_source=Sail-thru&utm_medium=email&utm_campaign=NR%20Daily%20Monday%20through%20Friday%202022-03-29&utm_term=NRDaily-Smart.

Kumar, Naveen. "Meet the Teens Telling Broadway 'What the Constitution Means to Me'" Teen Vogue, June 7, 2019. https://www.teenvogue.com/story/what-the-constitution-means-to-me?mbid=synd_yahoo_rss.

Lange, Jens, Lisa Blatz, Jans Crusius. "Dispositional envy: A Conceptual Review." Handbook of Personality and Individual Differences, (2018): 424-440. https://dx.doi.org/10.4135/9781526451248.n18.

Lange, Jens, Jans Crusius. "Dispositional Envy Revisited: Unraveling the Motivational Dynamics of Benign and Malicious Envy." Personality and Social Psychology Bulletin 41, No. 2 (February 2015): 284-294. https://doi.org/10.1177%2F0146167214564959.

Lindsey, Robert. "Family Tragedy: Hitler's Germany to Jones' Cult." New York Times, December 4, 1978. https://www.nytimes.com/1978/12/04/archives/family-tragedy-hitlers-germany-to-joness-cult-the-layton-familys.html.

Little, Laura E. "Envy and Jealousy: A Study of Separation of Powers and Judicial Review." Hastings Law Journal 52, No. 47 (2000). https://repository.uchastings.edu/hastings_law_journal/vol52/iss1/2.

Lott, Maxim. "10 Times 'Experts' Predicted the World Would End by Now." Fox News, March 19, 2019. https://www.foxnews.com/science/10-times-experts-predicted-the-world-would-end-by-now.

Miller, Matthew. "High School Teacher Fired After Praising Antifa: 'I Have 180 Days to Turn Them into Revolutionaries.'" The Washington Examiner, September 2, 2021. https://www.washingtonexaminer.com/news/antifa-supporting-high-school-teacher-revolutionaries.

Morgan-Knapp, Christopher. "Economic Envy." Journal of Applied Philosophy 31, No. 2 (May 2014): 113-126. https://doi.org/10.1111/japp.12045.

Bastian, Brock, Jolanda Jetten, Fabio Fasoli. "Cleansing the Soul by Hurting the Flesh: The Guilt-Reducing Effect of Pain." Psychological Science 22, No. 3 (January 18, 2011). https://doi.org/10.1177/0956797610397058

Patai, Daphne, and Noretta Koertge. Professing Feminism: Cautionary Tales from the Strange World of Women's Studies. New York: Basic Books. 1994.

Pluckrose, Helen, and James Lindsay. Cynical Theories. North Carolina: Pitchstone Publishing. 2020.

Poff, Jeremiah. "Ohio and Missouri School Board Associations Dump NSBA over Letter Calling Parents 'Domestic Terrorists.'" Washington Examiner, October 26, 2021. https://www.washingtonexaminer.com/restoring-america/community-family/ohio-and-missouri-school-board-associations-dump-nsba-over-letter-calling-parents-domestic-terrorists.

President and Fellows of Harvard University. The Black Book of Communism. Cambridge: Harvard University Press. 1999. https://www.hup.harvard.edu/catalog.php?isbn=9780674076082

Price, Robert. "NY Lawyers Plead Guilty to Firebombing Police Car During George Floyd Protest." Breitbart News, October 21, 2021. https://www.breitbart.com/law-and-order/2021/10/21/ny-lawyers-plead-guilty-to-firebombing-police-car-during-george-floyd-protest/.

Rand, Ayn. Atlas Shrugged. New York: Signet. 1992.

Rauschning, Herman. Hitler Speaks. New York: G.P. Putnam's Sons. 1940.

Rawls, John. A Theory of Justice. Cambridge: Harvard University Press. 1999.

Rosiak, Luke. "Teachers Compile List of Parents Who Question Racial Curriculum, Plot War on Them." Daily Wire, March 16, 2021. https://www.dailywire.com/news/

loudoun-teachers-target-parents-critical-race-theo-ry-hacking.

Rowan, Nic. "Ocasio-Cortez Compares Fighting Climate Change to Winning World War II." The Free Beacon, March 29, 2019. https://freebeacon.com/politics/ocasio-cortez-compares-fighting-climate-change-to-winning-world-war-ii/.

Ruiz, Michael. "Pro-Antifa California teacher to be fired by school district after leaked video emerges." Fox News, September 1, 2021. https://www.foxnews.com/us/pro-antifa-california-teacher-to-be-fired.

Salovey, Peter, Judith Rodin. "Coping with Envy and Jealousy." 7 Journal of Social and Clinical Psychology 7, 1 (January 2011). https://doi.org/10.1521/jscp.1988.7.1.15.

Savage Scharff, Jill, and Stanley A. Tsigounis, eds. Self Hatred in Psychoanalysis. New York: Brunner-Routledge. 2003.

Schoeck, Helmut. Envy, A Theory of Social Behaviour. Indianapolis: Liberty Fund, Inc. 1987.

Shapiro, Emanuel. "Dealing with Masochistic Behavior in Group Therapy from the Perspective of the Self." GROUP 25, (June 2001): 107–120. https://doi.org/10.1023/A:1011028909291.

Smil, Vaclav. National Library of Medicine, National Institutes of Health, December 18, 1999. https://www.ncbi.nlm.nih.gov/pmc/articles/PMC1127087/.

Snyder, Daniel, Maria Florencia Lopez Seal, Aaron Sell, Julian Lim, Roni Porat, Shaul Shalvi. "Support For Redistribution Is Shaped by Compassion, Envy, And Self-Interest, But Not a Taste for Fairness." Proceedings of the

National Academy of Sciences 114, no. 31 (July 2017): 8420-8425. https://doi.org/10.1073/pnas.1703801114.

Spacy, John. "Seven Examples of an Authoritarian Personality." Simplicable.com, May 5, 2020. https://simplicable.com/en/authoritarian-personality.

Thompson, Sherwood. *Encyclopedia of Diversity and Social Justice.* Maryland: Rowman & Littlefield Publishers. 2014.

Turley, Jonathan. "The Hitchhiker's Guide to CLS, Unger, and Deep Thought." Northwestern University Law Review 81, No. 4 (1987): 593-620.

U.S. Congressional Progressive Caucus, 2022. https://progressives.house.gov/.

Ulman, Richard B., D. Wilfred Abse. "The Group Psychology of Mass Madness." Political Psychology 4, No. 4 (December 1983): 637-661. https://www.jstor.org/stable/3791059.

Van de Ven, Niels, Charles E. Hoogland, Richard H. Smith, Wilco W. van Dijk, Seger M. Breugelmans, Marcel Zeelenberg. "When Envy Leads to Schadenfreude." Cognition and Emotion, 29, No. 6 (2015): 1–19. https://doi.org/10.1080/02699931.2014.961903.

Weber, Max. *The Protestant Ethic and the Spirit of Capitalism.* New York: Angelico Press. 2014.

Wolman, Benjamin B. ed., *International Encyclopedia of Psychiatry, Psychology, Psychoanalysis, and Neurology.* New York: Van Nostrand Reinhold Co. 1977.

Wulfson, Joseph. "Ocasio-Cortez Calls Climate Change 'Our World War II,' Warns the World Will End in 12 Years." Fox News, January 22, 2019.

https://www.foxnews.com/politics/ocasio-cortez-calls-climate-change-our-world-war-ii-warns-the-world-will-end-in-12-years

Yockey, Francis P. Imperium. Missouri: Invictus Books. 2011.

Zeigler-Hill, Virgil, Todd Shackelford, eds. SAGE Handbook of Personality and Individual Differences. Sage. 2018.

Endnotes

[1] Hawkins, "Remove Statues of Margaret Sanger, Planned Parenthood Founder Tied to Eugenics and Racism."

[2] And in fact, during the interwar period, tens of thousands of the "mentally insane," criminals, and others in the United States were forcibly sterilized. When this practice was finally outlawed in the U.S., the Nazis were only just ramping it up in their engineering ideal of an improved Aryan race, sterilizing Roma ("Gypsies") and other undesirables.

[3] The "Communist International" whose mission was to spread communism throughout the globe.

[4] Max Horkheimer is considered to have been the leader of the Frankfurt School. He had been appointed as Professor of Social Philosophy in Frankfurt and then Director of the Institute of Social Research. The Institute originated as a Marxist "study group," but shortly after Horkheimer's appointment, Hitler's Gestapo shut the Institute down. See the Stanford Encyclopedia of Philosophy at https://plato. stanford.edu/entries/horkheimer/ for a more in-depth discussion of Horkheimer and the Frankfurt School.

[5] Christie and Martin, *Jurisprudence*,

[6] Pluckrose and Lindsay, *Cynical Theories*.

[7] Christie and Martin, *Jurisprudence*,

[8] Turley, Jonathan, "The Hitchhiker's Guide to CLS, Unger, and Deep Thought."

[9] Bender, "A Lawyer's Primer on Feminist Theory and Tort."

[10] Ibid.

[11] Ibid.

[12] Turley, "The Hitchhiker's Guide to CLS, Unger, and Deep Thought."

[13] Pluckrose and Lindsay, *Cynical Theories.*

[14] Ibid.

[15] See generally, Patai and Koertge, *Professing Feminism, Cautionary Tales from the Strange World of Women's Studies.*

[16] "Social Justice" was coined around the 1880's by those who sought to establish pure equality in both American and European society.

[17] Jones, "Georgetown Students Reportedly Request Place to 'Cry' as Dean Addresses Ilya Shapiro's SCOTUS Tweets."

[18] Twitter Post: Pumpkin Spice Taryn, @aceinthehole, self-described " asexual writer, dramatic pisces, donut connoisseur, former sex blogger," 11/17/2021.

[19] University of Wisconsin-Milwaukee LGBT Resource Center in 2011

[20] Chak, "Beyond 'He' and 'She': The Rise of Non-Binary Pronouns."

[21] Dorman, "PBS Station Defends Drag Queen Skit for Kids: 'Performance Art That Can Inspire Creative Thinking.'"

[22] Barakat, "School System Pulls 2 Books with Graphic Sex from Libraries."

[23] National Association of School Boards, Letter September 29, 2021.

[24] de Beauvoir, *Ethics of Ambiguity.*

[25] Like most generalizations, this one is not free of exceptions: many Germans were opposed to socialism and the Nazi Party and its doctrine, although resistance to it varied from little more than shoulder shrugging to armed resistance groups engaged in passive or active operations against the Nazis.

[26] Fromm, *Escape from Freedom.*

[27] The unfounded premises assumed in this post aside (i.e., that the target audience actually "hated Rosa Parks" and the others for engaging in peaceful protest for what they felt was morally right), and the logical fallacy that because one supposedly "hates" other people for *their* actions, that one should hate oneself for *somebody else's* actions, were immediately challenged by others. While comments in opposition to the author's rhetorical question were varied and did not necessarily invoke the rules of formal logic, the word "psychosis" was used more than once to describe the mental state of the author. The use of this word by the general public to describe the Progressive's focus on "guilt" has increased proportionally as their social and political goals have recently attracted more attention.

[28] Ben-Zeev, "Envy and Inequality."

[29] Congressional Progressive Caucus website, 2022.

[30] President and Fellows of Harvard University, *The Black Book of Communism,*

[31] National Library of Medicine, National Institutes of Health.

[32] President and Fellows of Harvard University, *The Black Book of Communism*,

[33] Ibid.

[34] Bresanahan, Cheney, "Bizarre Fight Breaks out in House over Whether Socialists are Nazis." ("It's hard to listen to historical revisionism or perhaps ignorance about the Nazis," Nadler said admitting that the term Nazi was an acronym for the National Socialist German Workers Party.")

[35] President and Fellows of Harvard University, *The Black Book of Communism*.

[36] Ibid.

[37] Ibid.

[38] Rand, *Atlas Shrugged*.

[39] In fairness to Marx, his intent was an admirable one: to eliminate not only poverty but also the emotional "alienation" of modern, industrialized man, mainly by eliminating the pressure caused by his economic needs so he could become, in Marx's view, fully human. This is another failure of Marx's interpretation of human psychology, i.e., becoming "fully human" since a significant part of human existence is in the survival instinct. That is, *economic need* was and remains simply another form of the necessary preoccupation with human survival akin to hunting and/or gathering that has followed us through our genetic evolution until today. That need – to produce and to create in order to survive – is no less strong and no less essential to our becoming "fully human" than it was forty thousand or a million years ago. How we go about it, and how successful we are at providing for our economic needs is extraneous to our urge to do it.

40 Like future American author Ayn Rand's father, a medical doctor who, when Rand was just a young girl, they packed up their families and left for the West in what was likely the first "brain drain" as that term is used in post Enlightenment history.

41 The proponents of communist and fascist ideology, including Marx, were influenced by Hegel who pondered that man cannot be truly free until they surrender themselves completely to the state. A contradiction in any respect, but an idea appealing to the sadistic personality, that which defines both Lenin and Hitler, who seek to control the lives of others both for the emotional satisfaction of that control and toward whatever ends.

42 de Beauvoir, *Ethics of Ambiguity*.

43 Ibid.

44 Hoffer, *The True Believer,* (*quoting* Rauschning, Herman; Hitler Speaks, G.P. Putnam's Sons, 1940).

45 Hoffer, *The True Believer,*

46 And outlawed in half of the new states before the Civil War, beginning with Pennsylvania in 1778 whose legislature in that year adopted a phase-out plan that would end it completely by 1798.

47 Kurt Riezler, The Sociology of Fear, 1947.

48 Social media post, 2022, anonymous.

49 In May 2020, a Texas judge chastised a hair salon owner for not closing her business during the Covid pandemic because of, in the judge's words, "*some individual notion of freedom.*" The judge also stated that she owed her elected officials an apology and that she was "selfish" for putting her own interests (i.e., her income and her ability to feed

and clothe her own children) above the collective interests of the community. The judge's belief that freedom is anything, but an individual experience is highly disturbing but an example of how freedom is misunderstood even by those who are supposed to be trained in individual rights as found in the Bill of Rights of the Constitution – the source of *all* law in the United States. Freedom can *only* exist on the individual level.

[50] Not to downplay through nostalgic reflection, of course, the era's fair share of war, treachery, torture, crucifixion, famine, public games of mortal combat, deprivation of human rights and dignity, etc.

[51] We still refer to someone's passionate pursuit of a profession, vocation, or other life goal as "a calling," or with reference to religion, "a higher calling."

[52] Weber, *The Protestant Ethic and the Spirit of Capitalism.*

[53] Ibid.

[54] Fromm, *Escape from Freedom,*

[55] Johnston, *Why We Feel: The Science of Human Emotions,*

[56] Farnsworth, *The Practicing Stoic,* quoting Seneca.

[57] Johnston, *Why We Feel:*

[58] Snyder, "Support For Redistribution Is Shaped by Compassion, Envy, And Self-Interest, But Not a Taste for Fairness."

[59] Ibid.

[60] French Premier Georges Clemenceau (1841-1929).

[61] Delumeau, *Sin and Fear,*

⁶² Ibid.

⁶³ Ibid.,

⁶⁴ Envy is often confused with or in normal conversation often used interchangeably with the jealousy emotion. Jealousy, however, is different from envy and is quite its functional opposite. That is, the jealous person possesses something that he values highly and thus fears losing that thing to someone else. This seems most prominent with a love interest or significant other – boy or girlfriend, wife, husband, or partner – but it could be something else as well like position or prestige. Hence the phrase "to guard something jealously."

⁶⁵ Duffy, et. al. "A Social Context Model of Envy and Social Undermining."

⁶⁶ Ibid.

⁶⁷ "The Vision of Hell," Francisco De Quevedo: Dreams and Discourses, by Francisco De Quevedo and R. K. Britton, Liverpool University Press, 1989, pp. 90–179; (www.jstor.org/stable/j.ctv16zjxfc.7).

⁶⁸ Van de Ven, "When Envy Leads to Schadenfreude."

⁶⁹ Ashback,"Persecutory Objects, Guilt and Shame." (Self Hatred in Psychoanalysis).

⁷⁰ Lange, Jens & Blatz, Lisa & Crusius, Jan. (2018). Dispositional envy: A conceptual review. 10.4135/9781526451248.n18.

⁷¹ Duffy, et. al. A Social Context Model of Envy and Social Undermining, Academy of Management Journal, 2012

⁷² Scharff and Tsigounis, *Self Hatred in Psychoanalysis.*

[73] Rawls, John. A Theory of Justice. Cambridge: Harvard University Press. 1999.

[74] Snyder, "Support For Redistribution Is Shaped by Compassion, Envy, And Self-Interest, But Not a Taste for Fairness."

[75] Ibid.

[76] Women who identified with both parties were, interestingly, less supportive of wealth redistribution than men. This may be a matter of generalized "male *self-interest*" since, in at least American culture, men carry a heavier societal expectation to be the "provider" for their family, i.e., to get a job, blue-collar or otherwise; and when the family is not doing well financially it is still the male – notwithstanding women's accomplishments in the workplace–who people will tend to hold responsible first.

[77] Although the study did not ask participants if they identified with the Progressive movement, to what extent this decrease in charity by self-identified Democrats is related to Progressive Critical Race Theory is of interest. That is, the study showed more support for wealth redistribution by "Democrats" and the Progressive movement is, at least at present, inextricably linked to if not leading the Democrat party platforms. The Progressive notion is that charity is itself a racist concept and an act only meant to demean blacks by allowing white people to demonstrate their perceived superior socio-economic status by donating to the poor, which the Progressive associates with black Americans. See, for example, *The Unbearable Whiteness of American Charities*, Vox 7/1/2019 or as described by characters in Adija Adiches "anti-racist" novel *Amerikana*.

[78] Marcela García, *Why the Rich Should Pay More In Taxes*, Boston Globe, May 28, 2021

[79] Marcela García, *Why the Rich Should Pay More in Taxes,* Boston Globe, May 28, 2021

[80] Garcia, like many Progressives, appears to believe that wealthy people keep their money under their mattresses instead of with banks that lend money to people so they can purchase vehicles, homes, and other things that they deem essential, or by purchasing stock in companies that are calculated by economic theory to use the money exchanged to produce and grow business and industry, providing jobs for literally millions of job seekers in the nation. This rather than providing it to government, with its obvious lack of fiscal responsibility, and allowing the government to determine where money is best spent, a notion that never pays off for Garcia's "common good."

[81] Snyder, "Support For Redistribution Is Shaped by Compassion, Envy, And Self-Interest, But Not a Taste for Fairness."

[82] In an unprecedented act in May 2022, someone leaked a draft Supreme Court opinion authored by Justice Alito and purported to overturn the controversial 1970s Supreme Court decision in *Roe v. Wade,* which would relinquish abortion legislation back to the fifty states.

[83] Schoeck, *Envy: A Theory of Social Behaviour.*

[84] NY Lawyers Plead Guilty to Firebombing Police Car During George Floyd Protest, Breitbart News, 10/21/2021.

[85] Duffy, et. al. "A Social Context Model of Envy and Social Undermining."

[86] Ibid.

[87] Ibid.

[88] Sarah Jeong, "lawyer by training, journalist by vocation." 11/17/2021

[89] Ibid.

[90] Ibid. Social media has proven to be a significant asset in assessing the psycho-political makeup of the American Progressive, providing access to Progressive thoughts and ideas willingly contributed to the public square for scrutiny.

[91] Sarah Jeong, "lawyer by training, journalist by vocation." 11/17/2021

[92] Duffy, et. al. "A Social Context Model of Envy and Social Undermining."

[93] DeVega, "Dear Joe Biden: We Don't Want 'Unity' with Fascists — That's Why Democrats Lose." (Taney served as Chief Justice starting in 1836 and until his death in 1864 – just prior to the end of the Civil War).

[94] Schoeck, *Envy: A Theory of Social Behaviour*

[95] Ibid.

[96] Ibid.

[97] Lange, Blatz, Crusius, "Dispositional envy: A Conceptual Review."

[98] Kotkin. "The Most Dangerous Class. The Coming Revenge of the Disappointed

[99] Ibid.

[100] Fromm, *Escape from Freedom,*

[101] Ibid.

[102] The Economist, "Home Ownership is the West's Biggest Economic-Policy Mistake. It is an Obsession

that Undermines Growth, Fairness, and Public Faith in Capitalism." This article is so contrary to any sound economic or personal finance principle that, were it not taken from one of the West's most influential economic periodicals, it would be insignificant and not worth further attention.

[103] See, for example: Abraham, "The U.S. Needs a New Constitution to Address the Fundamental Wrong of Slavery."

[104] Duffy, et. al. "A Social Context Model of Envy and Social Undermining."

[105] Recall "dispositional envy," whether in reference to benign or malicious envy, refers to a quantitatively chronic condition. It is one in which the individual tends to experience envy across a variety of tasks and situations in life, and not just during otherwise isolated or occasional experiences of envy, viz., "episodic envy."

[106] Lange, Crusius. . "Dispositional Envy Revisited: Unraveling the Motivational Dynamics of Benign and Malicious Envy."

[107] Lange, Blatz, Crusius, "Dispositional envy: A Conceptual Review."

[108] Van de Ven, "When Envy Leads to Schadenfreude."

[109] Ibid.

[110] Little, "Envy and Jealousy: A Study of Separation of Powers and Judicial Review."

[111] Van de Ven, "When Envy Leads to Schadenfreude."

[112] Judicial Watch, "Montgomery County Schools Teacher Training Records Show Lessons on 'Restorative Justice' and 'Psychoeducation.'"

[113] Smithsonian Museum of African American History. "Aspects and Assumptions of Whiteness and White Culture in the United States." The content in the Museum's written exhibit was subsequently taken down by the curators: https://www.washingtontimes.com/news/2020/jul/17/smithsonian-african-american-museum-remove-whitene/

[114] Graham, John R. "The Constitution and Your 'Right to Health Care.'"

[115] Wulfson, Joseph. "Ocasio-Cortez Calls Climate Change 'Our World War II,' Warns the World Will End in 12 Years."

[116] "[h]e is compelled to conform, to seek his identity by continuous approval and recognition by others. Since he does not know who he is, at least the others will know, and he will know too, if he only takes their word for it."

[117] His doubt in his identity compels him to make, as de Beauvoir put it, "[n]ever positive choices, only flights," and in the reflection of the Collective "[h]e will proclaim certain opinions; he will take shelter behind a label; and to hide his indifference he will readily abandon himself to verbal outbursts or even physical violence. One day, a monarchist, the next day, an anarchist, he is more readily antisemitic, anti-clerical, or anti-republican."

[118] Hill Collins, Intersectionality (Key Concepts).

[119] Sherwood, Encyclopedia of Diversity and Social Justice.

[120] Spacey, "Seven Examples of an Authoritarian Personality."

[121] Spacey, "Seven Examples of an Authoritarian Personality."

[122] Perhaps the only exception is when one's child is the cause of a destructive act. A parent or guardian may feel some feeling of guilt indirectly for not having taken available steps in rearing the child that, had the child been taught

better, may have prevented the harmful act from occurring. However, with this type of harm through omission, causation may be quite speculative. The degree of any guilt emotion is not likely to be so powerful unless the omission has a more direct, causal link to the harmful act.

123 Hoffer, *The True Believer*,

124 Ibid.

125 Ibid.

126 Adams, "Seven Months Later, 1619 Project Leader Admits She Got it Wrong."

127 Hoffer, *The True Believer*,

128 Freud, *The Ego and the Id*.

129 Bastian, et. al. "Cleansing the Soul by Hurting the Flesh: The Guilt-Reducing Effect of Pain."

130 Ashback, "Persecutory Objects, Guilt and Shame." (Self Hatred in Psychoanalysis).

131 APA, *Diagnostic and Statistical Manual of Mental Disorders*

132 Ibid.

133 Ibid.

134 Ibid.

135 Shapiro, "Dealing with Masochistic Behavior in Group Therapy from the Perspective of the Self."

136 Wolman, Ed., *International Encyclopedia of Psychiatry, Psychology, Psychoanalysis, and Neurology*.

137 Depressive Masochistic Personality Disorder was identified as such in the DMV III. However, a highly

controversial decision was omitted from the DSM IV and subsequent versions, often now referred to as Self Defeating Personality Disorder.

[138] Duffy, et. al. "A Social Context Model of Envy and Social Undermining."

[139] See Naranjo, Ch. 3 Depressive Masochistic Personality Disorder.

[140] Ibid.

[141] Ibid.

[142] Wolman, Ed., *International Encyclopedia of Psychiatry, Psychology, Psychoanalysis, and Neurology.*

[143] Ben-Ze'ev, "Envy and Inequality."

[144] de Beauvoir, *The Ethics of Ambiguity,*

[145] Hoffer, *The True Believer,*

[146] Fromm, *Escape from Freedom,*

[147] APA, *Diagnostic and Statistical Manual of Mental Disorders*

[148] Ibid.

[149] Ibid.

[150] Fromm, *Escape from Freedom,*

[151] Character and Neurosis, Oliver P. John (Institute of Personality Assessment and Research, University of California), Citing Kelman.

[152] Miller, "High School Teacher Fired After Praising Antifa: 'I Have 180 Days to Turn Them into Revolutionaries.'"

[153] Ruiz, "Pro-Antifa California Teacher to be Fired by School District After Leaked Video Emerges."

[154] U.S. Supreme Court.

[155] Oliver P. John (Institute of Personality Assessment and Research, University of California), citing Harold Kelman.

[156] Ashback, "Persecutory Objects, Guilt and Shame." (Self Hatred in Psychoanalysis).

[157] Jones' appeal to paranoia here rings similar to DeVega's accusations that Republicans are as of March, 2022 planning "a society in which Black and brown people, to quote the infamous words of Chief Justice Roger Taney, have no rights the white man is bound to respect." (DeVega, "Dear Joe Biden: We Don't Want 'Unity' with Fascists — That's Why Democrats Lose").

[158] Lyndsey, "Family Tragedy: Hitler's Germany to Jones' Cult."

[159] Ulman, "The Group Psychology of Mass Madness."

[160] Ibid.

[161] New York Times, December 4, 1978.

[162] New York Times, December 4, 1978.

[163] Ulman, "The Group Psychology of Mass Madness."

[164] Ibid.

[165] Ibid.

[166] Ashback, "Persecutory Objects, Guilt and Shame." (Self Hatred in Psychoanalysis).

[167] Ibid.

[168] Ulman, "The Group Psychology of Mass Madness."

[169] Morgan-Knapp, "Economic Envy."

[170] Little, "Envy and Jealousy: A Study of Separation of Powers and Judicial Review."

[171] Ibid.

[172] Hoffer, *The True Believer*,

[173] Oddly enough, the frustration associated with not being able to create art was evident in many of the Nazi Party's top leaders, including Hitler. They had tried at one time or other in their lives to create artistic works but without talent, they failed. As the Third Reich grew in power and dominated Europe, they confiscated *en masse* historical works of art for themselves.

[174] Fromm, *Escape from Freedom*,

[175] Bernstein, *Dictatorship of Virtue*, p.

[176] Charles Louis Secondat, Baron de la Brède et de Montesquieu (1689-1755)

[177] This debate gave rise to the Three Fifths Compromise regarding slaves. Ironically, it was the southern or "slave colonies" that desired to count a slave as one whole person for purposes of determining the number of representatives in Congress, whereas it was the northern colonies, some of which were already in the process of outlawing slavery, or would soon after the forming the country outlaw it, that desired to count them as less than whole. That is, those who wanted the slaves to count as less than one person meant to keep the new slave states from having that much more power to preserve or increase it with federal authority in the years to follow.

[178] Chillizza, "Sorry, Hillary Clinton. The Electoral College Isn't Going Anywhere."

179 de Beauvoir, *Ethics of Ambiguity*, pp

180 Fearnow, "Joe Biden Says He'd Be the 'Most Progressive' President in History, Tells Bernie Sanders to 'Disown' Misogynistic Supporters."

181 From the author's conversations with Cuban exiles and family members.

182 Adolf Hitler, *Mein Kampf*. According to Fromm, "the fact that somewhere else [Hitler] declares that a boy should be taught to suffer injustice without rebelling," is a contradiction that is "the typical one for the sado-masochistic ambivalence between the craving for power and for submission."

183 It is obvious that this effort did not begin in 2020, but when many schools turned to distance/virtual learning during the Covid-19 lockdowns, many parents became more aware of what their children were learning and being taught. This resulted in social media and news outlet coverage of parental backlash.

184 Rosiak, "Teachers Compile List of Parents Who Question Racial Curriculum, Plot War on Them."

185 Poff, "Ohio and Missouri School Board Associations Dump NSBA over Letter Calling Parents 'Domestic Terrorists.'"

186 See for example, Zaretta, *Culturally Responsive Teaching and the Brain*.

187 Abraham, "The U.S. Needs a New Constitution to Address the Fundamental Wrong of Slavery."

188 Kumar, "Meet the Teens Telling Broadway 'What the Constitution Means to Me.'"

[189] Evans, *Dictionary of Quotations*, (quoting Lenin's Speech to Commissars of Education, Moscow, 1923).

[190] Schoeck, *Envy: A Theory of Social Behaviour*,

[191] Fromm, *Escape from Freedom*,

[192] Ibid.

CPSIA information can be obtained
at www.ICGtesting.com
Printed in the USA
JSHW021408290722
28582JS00002B/7